Praise for t

"A charming little travelogue where our writer opens a window to our enemy's house and discovers a home as haunted as ours."

– **Mohammad Hanif**, author of *A Case of Exploding Mangoes*

"Shueyb Gandapur had crossed continents before he decided to visit India. He takes us on a colourful guided tour of mosques, monuments, shrines, and temples, from the Taj Mahal to the ghats of Benares, from Ghalib's grave to a room that houses the belongings of Qurratulain Hyder. He encounters hostility and hospitality, religious differences and inclusiveness, and an end to certain preconceptions and prejudices which make him feel at once a sense of homecoming and a frequent estrangement. His gaze is both intimate in its celebration of old and new friendships, and clear eyed about the widening gap between the country of his birth and the land he longed to visit. His discoveries both in the erstwhile centres of Muslim culture and in the Hindu heartlands are often shot through with an abiding sense of wonder."

– **Aamer Hussein**, author of *The Cloud Messenger*

"Shueyb Gandapur's endearing travelogue begins with a child's yearning to visit a land he had heard about from his grandfather. He makes a cautious but nuanced foray into the space of 'neighbourly relations'— the highs and lows of the India-Pakistan relationship. Every vignette in this travelogue is engaging. The book is a page turner."

– **Mehr Afshan Farooqi**, author of *Ghalib: Flowers in a Mirror*

"Shueyb Gandapur's narrative is engaging and written with immense sensitivity. The author is a keen observer and displays empathy throughout his journeys. The divided Indian subcontinent has deprived the younger generations of South Asians to freely travel and interact. Aside from its descriptive merits, this book is an important addition to texts that defy borders guarded by nationalisms."

– **Raza Rumi**, author of *Delhi by Heart*

"Gandapur is a writer who is appreciably sensitive to the quality and texture of his interfaces and objective, historically nuanced and generous in the assessment of his impressions. In its natural and disarmingly everyday manner, the narrative neither lacks profundity nor wisdom. While identifying similarities and differences between Pakistan and India, he makes very interesting forays also to locate and contact the Derawal community in Delhi as well as the distinctive and largely forgotten Hindu Pashtuns. Chapters dealing with these themes are where the traveller's own unique and rich identity truly comes to the fore and hence the engagements that he describes are especially emotional and emotive. A palpable sensitivity and largesse permeate this book, as does a certain light-heartedness, wit and an appetite for sudden and unexpected romance."

– **Osama Siddique**, author of *Snuffing Out the Moon*

Coming Back

the odyssey of a Pakistani through India

Published by Countless Centuries Press 2025

First published in the UK by Kantara Press 2025
First published in Pakistan by Book Corner 2025

Cataloguing-in-Publication record for this book is available from the British Library

ISBN 978-1-0684508-0-8 (Paperback)
ISBN 978-1-0684508-1-5 (Hardcover)
ISBN 978-1-0684508-2-2 (E-book)

Cover painting by Shueyb Gandapur
Photographs by Shueyb Gandapur

Genres: 1. Travel. 2. Memoir. 3. India. 4. Subcontinent. 5. Non-fiction.

Coming Back

the odyssey of a Pakistani through India

SHUEYB GANDAPUR

COUNTLESS
CENTURIES
PRESS

To the forced migrants
who still hold on to the memories
of the homes they lost

Contents

Preface

WHEN I FIRST STARTED PUTTING THE RECOLLECTIONS OF MY VISIT TO India in writing, I had no idea that they would assume the shape of a book one day. Back in London, several months after my trip, I continued to revel in my memories of the country: its sights, smells and sounds. Those memories demanded to be written down, for they seemed too significant in my life's journey to be allowed to wear away with the corrosive forces of time. A journalist friend, who took very good care of me in Delhi, also insisted that I write down my impressions of his country with the offer of getting them published in a newspaper he worked for.

Like any modern-day traveller, I had brought back a sizeable repository of photographs, as well as some audio clips and a few random notes jotted down on my phone. But every time I thought to mould all of this raw material into a meaningful form, I reached an impasse. I realised that this was partly due to the restrictions that a long piece or a series for a newspaper or magazine placed on my writing. It was difficult to capture the breadth of what I experienced in India in such a narrow form.

Then came Christmas break the following year, and uncharacteristically, I had time off from work without any plans of using it to travel to a new country. This was when the reprimand of my conscience over my prolonged inertia became unbearable. I picked up my pen and let the ink flow. Flow it did, like a river that determines its own course. I do not know what came upon me, but I had never experienced such fluency in my writing before. The film of my trip to India started playing before my eyes. I kept on writing until I had recorded everything I remembered. When I finished, I heaved a sigh of relief as if a debt had been repaid. I sent the entire text to the journalist friend who had urged me to write. He responded with a promise that he would give it a read; a promise that might now get fulfilled, since the manuscript has acquired the form of a book.

Excerpts from this travel account were published in a literary journal and then it started gathering dust. A few years later, I attended a book launch in London at the insistence of a friend who was moderating a session with the author. The event that I was attending out of obligation to a friend turned out to be quite interesting for myself too. It was there that I had my first encounter with the publisher of Kantara Press. That chance meeting led to the idea to convert my travel account into a book.

When the idea of this book was initially discussed, I was not sure if I was qualified to author a book on this subject due to my brief visit of only two and a half weeks. This is, of course, not the first volume of its kind. Books about Pakistanis visiting India and vice versa have been written before. Writers have spoken about the similarities and familiarities they found in unlikely places. Some went on a quest to rediscover family roots, others tried to uncover the reality of everyday existence on "the other side" that is not reflected in media reports. But then I realised that my personal experience had its own place in time and history, distinct from the perspective and experience of everyone else, so why should it not be heard by the people of our two countries as well as the wider world?

As I now had a larger canvas to work with, I revisited the series and updated the narrative, unhindered by the restriction of a word count. Distance from the actual occasion of the visit bestowed me with further insights and interpretations. The detail I had to skip previously in the interest of brevity was reincorporated. A few months later, when I went back to my hometown, Dera Ismail Khan, wiser by the experiences gathered during my India trip, I looked at the crumbling houses, deserted temples and old neighbourhoods with more reverence and tenderness. They had once been inhabited and frequented by the city's Hindu and Sikh residents, who were uprooted during the chaos of Partition, and now lived hundreds of miles away, remembering and commemorating what they had lost. I felt like I had completed a circle and incorporated those later impressions in my account.

Relations between India and Pakistan are almost always characterised by varying degrees of mistrust and animosity with occasional efforts towards rapprochement, which rekindle overwhelming, although short-lived, feelings of warmth on both sides. The legacy of unresolved conflicts from the time of Partition has translated into four wars and many stand-offs that brought the two neighbours to the brink of war several times. At the time of my visit in the summer of 2017, the political climate was freezing cold and it has remained so, if not worsened, since then. This low period has lasted for longer than ever before during my lifetime. The forces of jingoism now act and speak with more confidence, drowning out voices calling for peace and free movement. Cross-border travel, which had picked up steam at the turn of the century, has almost dried up completely now.

I have tried to narrate my observations and impressions from many meetings and encounters in India about whether the adverse political climate between our two countries has had any effect on the attitudes and perceptions of ordinary people, about whether it is still possible, despite all the hurdles, to reach out and connect with each other based on our many cultural commonalities. What I saw and felt is told in the account that follows.

RJ-14
BM 4958

1

All the Reasons to Go to India

I HAD WANTED TO GO TO INDIA FOR SO LONG THAT I DON'T REMEMBER exactly when the desire took root in my heart. I must have been very young. Then again, as a child I had wanted to travel to every country of the world, despite this being a seemingly impossible dream in the world I grew up in. So, what was special about my longing to visit India?

Maybe the fact that it was demonised by those around me provoked some curiosity to discover what it was really like, or perhaps *know thy enemy* was a mantra I had imbibed from somewhere early on. My first introductions to that land were peppered with accounts of eternal animosity and ill-will existing between their people and mine, and thus "they" came to acquire an aura of exoticism and mystery. That mystery became even more alluring when I later discovered that the land I stood upon was once one with the land of "theirs".

But before recounting the details of what happened to me when I finally realised my dream and reached India, I feel compelled to go back to the beginning of the journey.

I am talking about growing up in the '80s in a city left far behind in the race towards modernity – the dry, dusty, remote town of Dera Ismail Khan in northwestern Pakistan. The arrival of the internet was still many years away but the technologies for entertainment that did exist, like the video-cassette recorder (VCR) for example, were not permitted in my ultra-conservative religious household, because they were frowned upon as instruments designed to destroy the moral fabric of our society. The device was believed to be part of a conspiracy which involved the screening of Indian film tape imports in unsuspecting homes in the remotest corners of Pakistan and thus polluting the land of the pure.

I was six or seven years old when I watched my first Indian film. It was at an uncle's house in Peshawar, where my family was on a visit. In his house, the VCR was not viewed as a weapon of mass moral corruption. Everyone was assembled in their living room around the small TV set (although it was not considered small in those days, because all TV sets used to be small back then) on which a videotape was playing. I remember the name of the film, "Mard" (Man). My older cousins referred to the hero as "Meetaab"- that's how my inexperienced ears captured the sound. Coming from a home with less permitting parents and having been exposed to nothing of the sort before, my mind as a child found the dances in the film a bit immodest and noticed that the characters spoke Urdu.

Since I believed that Urdu was an exclusively Pakistani language, which was completely distinct in speech and text from Hindi, I could not understand why it was spoken in an Indian film. For many years after that, I did not find a satisfactory answer to this question. Were the films made for Pakistanis or was the language of Indians same as Urdu? All the data I received in response to these questions, and subsequently about India in general, was very incoherent and confusing, further fuelling my quest to learn more and establish the truth.

A year or so later, when my parents returned from Hajj, a letter arrived for them after a few months. It was from an Indian family they had befriended during their holy pilgrimage that wanted to remain in touch. I had recently taken up the hobby of stamp collecting. The stamp on the envelope had "India" written on it in English and another script that I was told was Hindi. So, if their language was Hindi, which I could not read, why did they make films in Urdu? Again, I could not find a straightforward answer to this question.

All of this confusion prevailed, despite the fact that my maternal grandfather, our Babaji, had spent his childhood years in India. Inspired by nostalgia, he used to recount stories of what life was like in those years. His father and uncles had moved to some faraway corner of India from their equally far-flung native village, Kulachi (a town in district Dera Ismail Khan), in search of trading activities. God knows how many trades they would have tried their hand at before settling on the production and supply of a sealing resin cultivated in forests, called *lac*. Although it was all one country at the time, Babaji used to speak of India as if it were a foreign land even then.

One day he told us how he had travelled alone as an adolescent teenager from Dera Ismail Khan to join his father in India. It took him seven whole days and several modes of transportation to reach that nook of India where part of his family had established itself, while the other part remained in Kulachi. Due to the long distance and travel uncertainty, visits between the two family bases were few and far between.

Once, upon my inquiry, he told me the names of the cities in India where they had their family homes. The names were not the familiar ones I was expecting, like Delhi, Bombay, Calcutta or Madras, but strange and difficult to pronounce, so much so that I had to ask him to repeat several times to register them in my mind. Baikunthpur and Manendragarh, for example, were so obscure that I couldn't even find them in the world atlas book I had borrowed from a schoolmate, despite it having a detailed spread map of India. Babaji said that those cities were located in a princely state called Korea (not to be confused with the countries of the same name) ruled by a raja. It was a land where, as he reminisced, *sadhus* (Hindu ascetics) used to spend days on end in a single uncomfortable posture.

Many years later, when Google Maps arrived on the scene, I was able to find those two towns at last! To my surprise, they were pretty much on the other side of India and nowhere near where the current border of India and Pakistan lies. The towns of Baikunthpur and Manendragarh now fall within the boundaries of Chhattisgarh state. Babaji's seven-day land journey also started to make sense, but it made me wonder: What was the point of Babaji's father setting up base in a place that was just as remote and obscure as the place he had migrated from? Perhaps they were just following the time-honoured Pashtun tradition of travelling in the direction in which the sound of opportunity beckoned.

I often think about how my great-grandfather developed an acumen for such a specialised trade as the cultivation of *lac* and try to imagine how such economic prospects were identified and undertaken in the past. After Babaji's passing, I made more inquiries of elders in the family to confirm whether I remembered the stories told by him correctly and to obtain details I didn't manage to collect while he was alive. The snippets of forgotten family histories revealed to me had such a pull, that it seemed the past would forever keep me bound in its spell.

It turned out that trade in *lac* was just one of many professions my family engaged in, and just a continuation of the tradition of setting up new ventures in new lands from generations prior. My mother told me that Babaji's own maternal grandfather used to buy and sell elephants, a lucrative venture back then. My father told me his great-grandfather used to go to India with his stock of cloth, which he would sell on credit one season and return to collect his debts the next.

As far as Babaji's story was concerned, his father and uncle's business in Korea state thrived; they built three houses, invited their wives to join them, and produced children on the soil of India. One day, he told us the story of the car his father had bought. As it was the first car owned by a private person in the state, it attracted the admiration and envy of all and sundry, including the Raja. Family lore has it that one day the Raja sent his emissary to my great-grandfather, asking to borrow his car. It was a known fact that if the Raja borrowed something and liked it, it was unlikely to ever be returned. My great-grandfather was not willing to part with his prized possession and informed the Raja's emissary that the vehicle was out of order. This upset the Raja, who declared that if he could not use the car when he needed it, it would not be allowed to be driven on the mud roads of his princely state by anyone else either. In the face of this ban, the car was somehow smuggled out and sent to our native village, Kulachi. How the car made that long and arduous journey is not clear, but what was clear was that there was no one in Kulachi to drive it.

Years turned into decades and the car stood there in the backyard, rusting and rotting away. Chicken put it to good purpose by using it as their coop. For a long time, its metal parts were dismembered to repair other mechanical objects, until nothing remained of the machine. People from the village say that a nut or bolt from the car is still occasionally found by children playing in scattered debris, like bones from an ancient skeleton unearthed from the ground.

When the country was divided, my great-grandfather had to abandon all he had made in India to return to his native town. Some of his cousins and relatives, who had married Indian women stayed back. I am inclined to believe that some would have returned, leaving their Indian wives and children behind, because they refused to come along. No family link, however, remained intact between the leavers and stayers. The stream of letters exchanged in the years following Partition eventually dried up. Who at the time could have thought that the new frontiers erected between the two countries would prove to be so impenetrable?

While my great-grandfather was returning to his hometown as a result of Partition, there were those within his hometown who were leaving in the opposite direction. They were running towards a territory unknown, with no one to receive them and no place to seek shelter. I used to think that when I visit India, I would find out where they found shelter and ask them if they still remembered their Kulachi and Dera Ismail Khan, where their old, lovingly built homes became occupied by new immigrants.

Returning to the question of language, it was only during my early teens when satellite broadcasts were introduced and access to Indian content extended beyond Bollywood films, that I realised that what they spoke on TV and in films was Hindi, which sounded almost the same as Urdu, with the exception of Doordarshan news bulletins. If it was so similar to Urdu, why could I not learn to read its script? But who to learn it from was the real question. Internet had not yet arrived and finding Hindi guidebooks was next to impossible.

It was then that my quest for deciphering every letter of Hindi script started. I began to deconstruct the words I came across into what I perceived as individual letters, paid attention to their shapes, and attributed sounds to them based on trial-and-error to form words. The information available to me was gleaned from the Indian section of my collection of postage stamps and coins, along with the text that would flash for a blip on the TV screen at Babaji's house, for satellite TV was still not allowed into my house, being considered a source of moral depravity. Identifying sounds and forming words from a script that until then had been inaccessible to me was a joy of another kind.

While I found most words of Hindi and Urdu to be identical, some differences were noteworthy. I remember that on a postage stamp commemorating children's day, the Hindi text read '*Baal Din*', which was different from how it would be written in Urdu as '*Bachchon ka Din*' or more formal '*Youm e Atfaal*'. Yet the word *Baal* for children was not unfamiliar to me, as I had heard it used in Seraiki. Another worth noting difference was the plural of paisa, from the times when they had any worth: English text on Indian coins was the vernacular *paise* whereas on Pakistani coins, it was the anglicised *paisas*. Noticing these details was not only instructive about the evolution of formal Hindi and Urdu but also revealed influences from other regional languages. Around the same time, I was delighted to lay my hands on Indian stamps issued to honour Urdu poets like Allama Iqbal, Mirza Ghalib and Bahadur Shah Zafar, and one marking the arrival of 15th century of the Islamic Hijri calendar. Discovering these themes, that I considered closer to Pakistan, on Indian documents, contributed to building of a bridge in my mind that would transport me across the border one day.

Now that I look back, I think that by projecting my knowledge of Urdu vocabulary to educate myself about the Hindi script and discovering familiar religious and linguistic references in this journey, I inadvertently embarked on an inquiry into the common ethos of Hindustani culture. I learned from the enchanting stories of Qurratulain Hyder later in life that this culture was called Ganga-Jamuni Tehzeeb – a syncretic fusion of Hindu and Muslim cultural elements.

Hence, I thought I would go to India one day to experience what was left of that Tehzeeb, to find traces of my hometown in the streets of Delhi and to ascertain whether *sadhus* still maintained one posture for days on end. I discovered a lot more in my pursuit than I had set out to find, the details of which follow in the ensuing pages.

की हार्दिक शुभकामनाएं!
अजय नारायण यादव

2

Be Careful What You Choose

IT IS NO SECRET THAT NEITHER INDIA NOR PAKISTAN MAKE IT EASY FOR the citizens of each country to visit the other. In fact, their visa policies make such visits quite a daunting undertaking. This is why, despite sharing the same subcontinent, my turn to visit India came after I had visited twice as many countries as my age.

For the average Pakistani, the thought of applying for an Indian visa is quite intimidating. Stories of visa rejection far outnumber those of success, which deters many aspiring travellers from even attempting to apply. However, the time finally came when I resolved to stop making excuses and start making sincere attempts to secure my passage to India. I prepared myself for all the additional requirements that Pakistani visa applicants have to fulfil, including providing one's family history dating back more than a couple of generations, to the repetitive police reporting and restriction of movement within select cities.

A few weeks after having applied for the visa at the Indian High Commission in London, I received a call one fine afternoon from a woman from the Consular section. After the standard confirmation of identity, the conversation followed thus:

"Choose any four cities," she said in a commanding tone.

"But the High Commission's website said I could choose up to five!" I made a feeble attempt to ask for more.

"That may be so, but you'll be given a visa for only four cities. If you want it, you have to choose those cities now."

It was clear that there was no further room to manoeuvre. I had to make up my mind on the spot about which city to drop out of the five I had listed on the application form and be grateful that I was on the verge of receiving a visa after all.

However, the woman on the phone refused to confirm whether my visa application had been successful. In fact, she specifically said that her call did not mean that the visa was going to be granted. Still, my hopes rose high – otherwise, why would she ask me to choose four cities? The long dreamed of visit to India was soon going to become a reality.

It was a hard choice to decide which of the five cities to sacrifice. In fact, I had sneakily listed a sixth one, namely Gurgaon, because I was unsure whether permission to visit Delhi encompassed Gurgaon as well, and I was keen to visit a friend's house there. To gain time, I asked the lady if she could remind me which cities I had applied for.

"Delhi, Agra, Jaipur, Varanasi, Lucknow, Gurgaon."

"Delhi… Agra… Jaipur… Varanasi… Luc…." I repeated the names slowly, thinking out loud.

"Done, thank you," she said before cutting the call, and thus the axe fell on Lucknow and Gurgaon.

स्वागतम्
शुभ
लाभ

3

The Visiting Neighbour Registers Himself

IT WAS A SWELTERING DAY IN JUNE WHEN I ARRIVED AT THE INDIRA Gandhi International Airport in Delhi. A sign in Hindi in the arrivals lounge greeted the newcomers and returners, "*Bharat mein aapka swagat hai*" (You are welcome in India). I hoped the immigration officers would make me feel welcome too.

As I handed over my Pakistani passport at the immigration counter, the officer on the other side seemed rather unhappy for the extra work that had just landed on his shoulders. Without saying a word, he got up and went from counter to counter searching for something in the drawers. He came back, bringing a pile of papers, settled in his chair and started to neatly arrange the white paper sheets alternating with black carbon paper. He handed the pile to me with the instruction to fill them with my particulars.

The details asked for on the form were no different from what I had provided at the time of visa application. Bureaucratic love for excessive paperwork is widespread in the subcontinent. Upon filling in the forms, my passport was stamped (to my great relief) and I was inside Indian territory in no time. I remember feeling thrilled and still quite unable to believe I had made it to Indian soil.

Driving from the airport to the hotel in a cab with my designer friend, Arunav Gogoi, whose house I had wanted to visit when I listed 'Gurgaon' on my visa application, I was pleased to notice Urdu on the multilingual road signs that also included English, Hindi and Punjabi. We arrived at the hotel near Connaught Place, where I had booked a room. The check-in process took rather long. The lady at the reception took my Pakistani passport to her manager to make sure it was okay for the hotel to host me, an experience that was repeated at every hotel in every city I stayed in, and included a cancellation from one hotel in Agra that did not want to deal with the hassle of police registration matters for Pakistani guests.

Since the visa I was granted required police reporting in every city, I proceeded to the relevant office near the Ajmeri Gate area of Old Delhi. I was surprised to find a purpose-built, large office building with a sign outside that read 'Pakistani Visitors Registration Office'. I initially wondered whether the number of visitors from Pakistan was large enough to warrant a whole facility dedicated to them, but I soon found out that that was not the case.

Only a couple of other men were waiting to be attended to, but they didn't look Pakistani to me.

The registration office was a decent-sized hall, with plastic benches on one side and counters with glass barriers on the other. Only two counters were manned. A TV set attached to the wall played a news channel broadcast with multiple tickers running across the bottom of the screen. The presenter was agitatedly reporting the news of a gang rape incident on repeat. One of the men in the hall commented, "The only solution is to castrate these culprits; only then will such incidents come to an end." The policeman sitting behind the glass counter laughed incredulously. "That will turn half the men in the country into eunuchs. How many will you castrate?"

When my turn came, I presented my papers, answered questions about the purpose of my visit and the address of my stay, hoping nervously that my answers satisfied the officer. Everything seemed to be in order until the police officer asked for Form-C, which is supposed to be issued by the hotel at which one is staying. Despite having done a lot of homework about the documentation requirements, I had not come across any mention of this particular form. I went back to the hotel, hoping against hope that the people there would be aware of what this form was about and how to get it.

After another hour's wait at the hotel – an hour that was used to have lunch at the restaurant, where we were served by a waitress who told me that she was from the North-east, just like Arunav, the Assamese friend I was having lunch with – I received my Form-C, went back to the registration office and heaved a sigh of relief once the whole process was complete. My stay in India was now fully compliant—at least for the first few days. The registration needed to be renewed before leaving and upon arriving in every city.

I celebrated this milestone by going to a nearby roadside tea stall and downing a few cups of cutting chai. Over the following two weeks, the number of cups of chai I consumed from tea-stalls and *dhabas* (kiosks) must have run into the hundreds. Never mind the high temperatures of summer; my hot beverage of choice was in abundant supply and consuming it was my favourite activity.

I visited the police registration offices ten times in four cities to register my arrival and departure in each city. Luckily, I did not have to wait long at any of them. Minus Delhi, I did not find any other Pakistani visitors waiting to be registered. What was on the one hand a boon for me as I didn't have to wait in queues was on the other hand, a sad indication of the number of Pakistani visitors in India.

In each city, the registration officers did their job as a routine affair without appearing inquisitive or curious. They noted down my details in thick dusty notebooks retrieved from piles of files and folders. The only hint of curiosity was shown by an officer in Jaipur. Seeing my place of birth, Dera Ismail Khan, on my passport, he asked in Hindi, "Is this birthplace of yours some sort of a *dera*?" (*Dera* is an Urdu/Hindi word meaning an encampment or abode).

Though generally thought of as a hassle, for me, watching the goings-on inside the old *thaana* buildings, the conduct of the policemen and intelligence officers with each other, other visitors, and with me, was fascinating. The world of police stations worked at a leisurely pace, under whirring ceiling fans. The thick dusty notebooks had records of hundreds of thousands of visitors jotted down in them with the liquid ink of fountain pens. I wondered if those records would ever be retrieved from those registers for any purpose.

Near the end of my India trip, when I went to the foreigners' registration office in Delhi to register my departure, I was surprised to overhear two gentlemen in Sikh turbans conversing in Pashto. Intrigued by the sound of my native language in Delhi, I went over to them to ask them where they were from and what they were doing there. We exchanged pleasantries warmly. They were uncle and nephew, hailing from Peshawar, who had come to India as asylum seekers. The uncle had been living in India for the past 7 years, but the nephew had only arrived a year ago. He was there to register his departure. Due to the difficulties arising from an uncertain legal status, as well as longing for his hometown, he had given up on making India his adopted home. In comparison, living in his native Peshawar was more familiar and less hassle, although less safe for him than it used to be.

The continuing stream of Pakistani Hindus and Sikhs migrating to India is a sorry reflection of their alienation from their home country. Upon departure, my Sikh compatriot invited me to his house in the neighbourhood of Lajpat Nagar. With his palm on his chest, he said in Pashto, "*Ka mung da para sa khidmat vi, nu hukam kawa.*" (If we can be of any service to you, then you just have to command us).

بسم الله الرحمن الرحيم
प्रो. अब्दुल खालिद
الله
दिलखुश टी स्टॉल
जी मौ. सुल्तान जी चाय वाले
दِल خوش ٹی اسٹال
नं. 5985, बल्लीमारान, दिल्ली-6
नसीम

4

Exploring Selected Indian Cities... Within Limits

PERHAPS IT WAS A BLESSING IN DISGUISE THAT I WAS ALLOWED TO VISIT only four cities because the time I had was barely enough to scratch the surface of the permitted destinations. Maybe the Indian High Commission in London also wanted me to leave some cities for future visits. But how many future visits would be needed to cover the vastness that is India?

Then there was the question of where a city's boundaries began and where they ended. Did Delhi mean all of National Capital Region (NCR) or was my permission restricted to the limits of the union territory of Delhi? Did my permission to visit Agra include Fatehpur Sikri? Could I sneak out from Jaipur to make a day trip to Ajmer Sharif if I returned by nightfall? My entry papers clearly stated that setting foot in the cantonment areas was prohibited for Pakistani citizens, but how could I work around the fact that the main train station in Agra, the point of my arrival and departure in the city, was situated *in* the cantonment area?

To clarify such confusions, I sought guidance from the officer at the foreigners' registration office in Delhi. I asked him if I could go to Gurgaon, a city in the neighbouring state of Haryana, but part of the ever-expanding NCR spreading around Delhi. He had some words of deep wisdom to offer. With a look directed straight at me, as though he was sizing me up, he asked, "So many thefts and robberies happen every day. How many of the thieves do you think get caught?"

I held my breath in silence, waiting for him to answer his own rhetorical question.

"If you are planning to commit a theft, make sure you don't get caught."

Taking a conservative estimation of the permissions around my movements, I started my exploration of Delhi from Raisina Hill.

Also known as Lutyen's Delhi (after the British architect who designed most of New Delhi's buildings during the Raj times) it houses India's most important government offices. On the road leading to the Secretariat buildings, I came across a dry fountain lit by electric lights in the colours of the Tricolour (India's national flag). The fountain's dryness was not on account of any fault in its functioning but because I visited it outside its "operating hours", which were clearly and boldly displayed on a sign beside it.

I had been advised to look for the inscription on the North Block of the Secretariat building that read "Liberty will not descend to a people; a people must raise themselves to liberty. It is a blessing which must be earned before it can be enjoyed."

The building was inaugurated in 1927 and the irony was that the inscription appeared to be a challenge to the local people by the British Raj to fight for their own freedom from colonial occupation instead of expecting it to be delivered to them on a platter. How intriguing it is then, that within two decades of the launch of one of the grandest projects of its time – the construction of a complex consisting of the Viceroy's House (currently Rashtrapati Bhavan), the House of Parliament, both blocks of the Secretariat and the nearby India Gate monument – which aimed to reflect India's centrality in the British colonial empire, India won its freedom, thus succeeding in the challenge presented to its people.

India Gate is located a short distance away. It was originally built as the 'All India War Memorial' to remember the soldiers of the British Indian Army who died fighting for the Empire in different parts of the world. Like a traveller who is delighted to find any reference to his homeland, I found one such reference to the North-West Frontier region (now the Khyber-Pakhtunkhwa province of Pakistan) engraved on India Gate. It read, "… in sacred memory also of those whose names are here recorded and who fell in India or the North-West Frontier and during the Third Afghan War."

How is it that the North-West Frontier was mentioned in addition to India, though it was part of India? Was it that just like in Babaji's days, when they travelled between their village in the North-West and the central Indian territories of Chhattisgarh, they used to refer to the latter as India, and perceived themselves to be separate from it, though cognisant of being a part of it at the same time? By the same token, maybe the feeling of "otherness" toward the North-West was reciprocated by the central government of India.

The area surrounding India Gate was buzzing with crowds, mostly comprising of domestic tourists, many of whom were probably visiting for the first time. I was not the only one. Men and women from the provinces were dressed up for the occasion, to be photographed against the backdrop of this landmark monument. I wondered why I hadn't made more of an effort, considering it was as much of a big deal for me, if not bigger, to be at India Gate.

Lots of portable stalls and carts were being pushed around through the crowds, selling sweets and snacks. Arunav, who had been accompanying me, suggested we let one of the young photographers touting his Polaroid take our photo at India Gate. I welcomed his suggestion. In the vast grounds around the imposing monument, filled to the brim with people, I texted another old Indian friend in New York, saying, "I have never seen so many Indians in my life."

"What did you expect?", quick came her reply.

The following day, I headed towards the old city of Delhi. The auto rickshaw, which in compliance with Indian naming conventions, will be called just 'auto' from here onwards, dropped me by what seemed like a massive rubbish heap. The atmosphere was bustling with a sense of disorder. Arunav had joined me again. Starting from Chandni Chowk, we made our way through the narrow lanes of the old city to reach Paranthe Wali Gali. I wanted to go there because in a flight of fancy, a former romantic liaison in London, who derived half of her DNA from India, had promised to wait for me on the night of a full moon, in a corner of this famed street, behind the green wooden door of a house that had 786 (a number South Asian Muslims associate with the Islamic phrase '*bismillah ir rahman ir raheem*') engraved on it. It was neither night nor were there any prospects of a full moon showing up, yet walking those streets carried a sense of fantasy and possibility. I just followed the aroma of parathas.

Contrary to what the name suggested, there were not a whole lot of paratha outlets in that street. While we lurked in the street contemplating which paratha place to favour, a server from one of the cafés, who had been eyeing our prolonged state of indecision, called out, "*Bade dinon baad aaye!*" (It took you so long to come back!)

The sense of belonging and familiarity encapsulated within that sentence disarmed me. It might have been merely said for the sake of luring a customer to the shop, but there was also something sincere and profound about it. The streets of old Delhi could have recognised me as the person whose imaginations had been visited by ideas of a rendezvous under the shadow of its walls. "*Bade dinon baad aaye*" became the mantra of my whole India sojourn.

A first-time visitor from Pakistan being greeted with the mistaken familiarity of an old-time city resident showed me that decades of barriers might have allowed mutual estrangement to deepen its roots, but on occasion it seemed that those barriers have failed to diminish the connection between the people of the region that goes back many, many centuries. My decision had been made for me. I walked into his café.

By this time, I had consumed several cups of chai. Sometimes it was served in small glass tumblers, known as "cutting chai" cups, and at other times, in cups made of unglazed clay called *kulhad* – both without loop handles to hold them. These tea-serving containers were quite different from those I had seen used in Pakistan at tea-stalls, *dhabas* or restaurants, where tea is almost always served in 'handled' porcelain mugs or cups with saucers. In Peshawar and surroundings, however, green tea (*qehwa*) is served in handle-less small cups.

I found it strange that the clay cups were thrown away after only one use. I thought they could be easily washed and used again. It reminded me of a passage from Ahmed Ali's novel, *Twilight in Delhi*, which was one of the books I had read ahead of my visit:

"But still a few shops of the milk-sellers are open, and someone comes and buys a couple of *pice* worth of milk, drinks it, and throws the earthen cup away to be licked by cats who steal out of dark corners."

The practice of drinking in clay cups and throwing them away had remained unchanged through the century between the era depicted in the novel and my visit to the city. The unglazed clay cup is said to infuse the taste of tea with an earthy flavour. With the introduction of cheaper alternatives such as disposable paper or polystyrene cups, *kulhads* retain their status as containers brimming with charm. Perhaps they are kinder to the environment too, as in the process of their disposal, earth returns to earth. Historically, they were the cheaper containers for serving tea, but these days, they are being reintroduced in fancier desi cafés around the world.

Going back to the narrow lanes of Old Delhi, I observed plenty of carved wooden doors, windows with iron bars, *jharoka* balconies and hole-in-the-wall shops, I could see why it was compared with the walled city of Lahore. At the same time, I asked myself how those winding lanes, those houses made of narrow brick, those entrance portals with niches for lamps, and those hand-painted nameplates were different from those I had seen in my own hometown, Dera Ismail Khan.

5

Further Forays into Older Delhis

FROM THE FAMILIAR LOOKING AND SMELLING LANES OF OLD DELHI, I moved towards the grandiose *Laal Qila* (Red Fort) nearby. The most well-known reference to *Laal Qila* I had come across prior to visiting it was the repeatedly expressed daydream of the jingoistic zealots in Pakistan about hoisting the Pakistani flag atop it one day. And now here I was, approaching the sprawling estate of the former Mughal royal court, with India's tricolour flag proudly fluttering over its huge entrance.

On the way to Laal Qila, I passed by a roadside vendor selling knickknacks. Taking me as a visitor from abroad, he called out in English, asking me where I was from. When I answered, "Pakistan", his curious reaction was to raise a slogan, "I love my India!" Surprised and amused, I smiled and moved on. Passing the same street in a cycle rickshaw later that day, the same vendor caught sight of me once more and shouted, "Mr. Pakistani!" I waved at him from the rickshaw. He immediately took out a cap from his merchandise spread out on the ground and put it on his head. "I love my India," he repeated. The cap that he put on sported a logo, which I paid little attention to at the time, but my friend later told me was of the ruling political party, BJP.

On reaching Laal Qila, the first thing I observed was that the main entrance of the fort retained the name 'Lahore Gate', because it led to or faced the other most important city of Mughal India, Lahore. After passing through the main gate, one enters a covered bazaar called Chhatta Chowk. It is lined with souvenir shops on both sides. Despite being deep inside Laal Qila, the arched Chhatta Chowk gave the appearance of a regular bazaar where people had come to look for their everyday needs. It is said that during the Mughal era it was a very exclusive shopping centre pandering to the luxurious tastes of the upper classes, selling expensive fabric, and jewellery of gold and precious stones. When I visited, the shops were offering cheap gifts and souvenirs to tourists from the provinces and further afield. Stray dogs lay calmly in the middle of the path with their eyes closed, not worried about the risk of their tails being stepped upon by some inattentive visitor. Emerging on the other side of Chhatta Chowk, I found a sign that I read with pleasure because it referred to the region I came from:

"Chhatta Chowk means covered bazaar, which in the 17th century India was extremely unusual and this one especially is unique in Mughal architecture. The notion of a covered bazaar was stimulated by the one Shah Jahan saw in Peshawar in 1646 (now in Pakistan)."

With the trend of changing names of historical places gathering pace in India, one wonders if these names and references will survive. Inside Laal Qila, there were many chambers and apartments, emperors' courts for the public and for the elite, several gardens, fountains, and a three-domed mosque with white marble interior, all fully ornamented. In short, it contained everything you would expect in a grand Mughal architectural project, representing the best of its creativity and blending Persian, Timurid and Indian influences.

A part of the Red Fort complex has been converted into an archaeological museum, where I saw two young men, hands on each other's shoulders, taking selfies under a warning sign prohibiting photography.

The two grand architectural masterpieces of Mughal Delhi, Laal Qila and Jama Masjid, find their equivalent in almost identical structures in the other erstwhile capital of the empire, Lahore. I left Laal Qila and made my way towards Jama Masjid. I was fully cognisant of the risk of overdosing on Mughal creative accomplishments within a short space of time, but I was about to realise that India was a land of overdoses and it was only my first full day of exploration.

Before reaching the Jama Masjid, I passed through a marketplace on the way. There was a signboard announcing its name as 'Meena Bazaar', but it lacked the hustle and bustle to deserve a mention in the *Kajra Mohabbat Wala* song. I couldn't help thinking of Indian music and film references to all the places I was visiting. Maybe Meena Bazaar was past its glory or maybe there was another more interesting one in the past.

When I turned to Google, it said that the Chhatta Chowk in Laal Qila that I had just come from was also known as Meena Bazaar, whereas the place where I was standing was identified variously as Kabootar Market (Pigeon Market), Chor Bazaar (Market of Thieves) and Kabadi Market (Scrap Market).

Regardless of the name, business was slow that afternoon, and I saw shopkeepers lounging in their chairs inside their shops, without actively soliciting customers. On top of that, it was the month of Ramzaan. A couple of them were reading Quran quietly under the siesta-inducing air of ceiling fans.

I reached the grand Masjid-e-Jahan-Numa (the original name of Jama Masjid) and was awed by the magnificence of its façade. On a very hot June afternoon, I burned my feet walking on its white marble floor but cooled my eyes with the views of the city after climbing the many stairs of one of its minarets. In the viewing galleries of the minarets, one can truly appreciate the perfection of the mosque's enormous and shapely domes. I spent a long time there taking in the views and resting after having done a good deal of walking.

The topmost viewing gallery was big enough to accommodate several people. I had the company of three boys that I kept watching as they took pictures from every possible angle. When one of them seemed to have had enough and asked to go downstairs, another from the group responded, "Hold on, we have paid 15 rupees for the ticket, so let's stay until we have had our money's worth of views." I asked that guy to take a photo of me against the background of the densely built old quarters of Delhi, visible through the lattice grille of the viewing chamber. Satisfied with the photo, I realised that I had gained more than my ticket price's worth and decided to go down.

I spent some time in the prayer hall below, where some people were resting, some praying and some gathered in circles to chat. A couple of them greeted me and asked me where I had come from. The expressions were welcoming after hearing my answer.

Time to leave, I found myself exiting from a different gate of the mosque than the one I had entered. Right outside this gate, further down the steps, I noticed two small structures that looked like shrines, striking due to their bright paint, one red, one green. When I came closer, I read the signs inscribed in Urdu on each of them. The green one was the dargah of Khwaja Syed Abul Qasim Hare Bhare Shah (the Evergreen One) and the red one was the dargah of Sufi Sarmad Shaheed. The name struck me. I had heard this name many years ago. Sarmad Shaheed.

It took me back 28 years to when I was a little kid at school. My schoolteacher had told the class a story of one Shaheed. Was it the same Sarmad Shaheed whose tomb I was standing before? My teacher's story was devoid of details of time and place, or perhaps I had forgotten them over time, but the account I could retrieve from my memory included the spectacle of an extraordinary miracle performed by Sarmad Shaheed. According to my teacher, he was a saint who had attained a status reserved for people bestowed with divine favour. "*Pohanche huay buzurg*" was the Urdu term she used, meaning a holy man who has arrived. Where? There, where only a select few can.

Sarmad had embarked on a spiritual journey in search of divine truth. Being inclined towards religious syncretism, he had shunned conventional rituals and roamed around naked in the streets of Delhi. This practice might have been inspired by the banishment of all worldly possessions, as observed by some Jain and Hindu ascetics. The royal court summoned him to explain his nonconformist ways. Sarmad refused to toe the official line, and at the risk of forfeiting his life, he demonstrated absolute devotion to his inner truth. The court charged him with heresy for which death was the punishment.

He was beheaded by the strike of a sword right outside the Jama Masjid. What followed next was something that caused a commotion amongst the gathered crowd. Sarmad's headless body rose and clutched its severed head in its own two hands. Holding the head in its hands, the body started walking towards the spot where the emperor sat on his throne. The crowd was dumbstruck. From amongst them, a holy man with a white flowing beard came forward, raised his hand to stop Sarmad and said sternly, "Enough! You have made your point. Now let nature take its course."

That holy man was Khawaja Hare Bhare, Sarmad's spiritual guide. If Sarmad continued his miraculous march after death, a bigger calamity might have befallen the empire, causing much destruction.

Thinking back to the memory of that legend told by my teacher, I realised I was standing on the steps of Jama Masjid where blood dripping from Sarmad's severed head must have made a trail, as he carried it in his hands to enter the mosque's courtyard. The message of the story was: Do not judge the piety of people based on their outward appearance, for they may be closer to God than those who condemn them. The state of hearts is known only to God. It bore the simplicity and magic of a fable.

That same Sarmad, the rebel, the martyr, now lies buried in the shadow of Jama Masjid next to Khawaja Hare Bhare. His tomb is red, and his teacher's tomb is green, representing martyrdom and immortality. The remarkable thing about South Asian Islam is that the tomb of a mystic who gave up all outwardly displays of piety is now a pilgrimage site adorned with Quranic verses, where devotees come and pray and hope for their wishes to be fulfilled.

Later that day, I went on to visit another minaret in another part of Delhi: The marvel called Qutub Minar from the times of Delhi Sultanate, predating the Mughal empire, which stands as an independent structure in Mehrauli. Unlike the minarets of Jama Masjid, climbing this one was not allowed. The tower was inscribed with beautiful calligraphy in Persian and Arabic. It's a monument unique in design and said to be the earliest and best example of synthesis of Indic and Islamic traditions. For me, the most surprising find was the carved motifs on the decorated pillars of the adjacent Quwwat-ul-Islam Mosque, which depicted sculpted figures of Hindu gods and goddesses. Built in the late 12th and early 13th century, the minaret and the nearby mosque were constructed by Hindu labourers and craftsmen but overseen by Muslim architects.

I later learned that the mosque had been built with remnants of Hindu and Jain temples. Considering that representations of human and animal forms are generally forbidden in mosques, one would assume that either the job of defacing them was not properly done, or the plaster used to cover them had fallen off over the centuries, as has happened in several converted churches, pharaonic temples and mosques in other parts of the world.

On the one hand, the whole Qutub Minar complex remains a testament to the incredible architectural and aesthetic prowess of the early sultans of Delhi, some of whom lie buried in their tombs within the same complex, and on the other hand, it is also a reminder of how materials from demolished indigenous places of worship were used to build grand monuments to mark the victory of the new conquerors.

Indira Gandhi International Airport is not too far from Qutub Minar, so in the vast open space, one could see planes flying overhead from time to time. This gave me the silly idea of capturing a flying plane, the Qutub and myself in the same shot. The execution of the idea was a success; however, when I now look at the photo, it appears that the plane is heading straight into the tower, bracing for an enormous collision. What other thought could come to one's mind seeing an aeroplane and a tall building in the same frame in this day and age?!

My entire visit to India happened during the month of Ramzaan, which is a festive time in Old Delhi, especially at night when its streets come alive. People come out to eat or just roam the streets and shop for the upcoming festival of Eid, after being energized by the iftar meal, the breaking of the fast at sunset. The area was buzzing with men, some of them donning Muslim skullcaps, and women, some of them in burqas. On the walls were plastered Hindi and Urdu posters by local politicians from AAP, Congress and BJP wishing their Muslim brothers and sisters a blessed Ramzaan and happy Eid. One could get carried away by a feeling of communal harmony.

Other than the posters, I came across *khatna* (circumcision) clinics manned by grim reapers sitting behind time-beaten wooden counters that must have held their scary-looking blades. Right next door was another shop full of blades and knives. It was a meat shop, with a sign announcing the price of a leg and a breast. In the lanes, baby mannequins in garment stores were dressed in kurta pajamas, kebab and jalebi shops emitted mouth-watering aromas, many signboards in Urdu displayed special discounts for Eid, and one restaurant offered "Lahori food".

A bit further on, a sign on a huge banyan tree depicted a painting of a *pehlawan* (traditional wrestler) beneath the image of the Kaaba. The Urdu text on the sign read: *Here, broken bones and other such injuries are treated satisfactorily*. In the streets of Old Delhi, at every turn, a new object of curiosity awaits.

I visited more of the usually frequented monuments from the times of the Delhi Sultanate and Mughal India. Even after the passage of centuries, the prominent ones among them still look so majestic. Humayun's Tomb was a feast for the eyes. Safdarjang's Tomb, with its serene atmosphere and imposing domed structure surrounded by beautiful well-kept gardens, became my favourite. However, in Mehrauli, right outside the dargah of Hazrat Khawaja Bakhtiyar Kaki, there was a beautiful structure of typical Mughal style of construction in a very decrepit state. I later learnt its name was Zafar Mahal, and it was built when the last remaining signs of Mughal rule were well within sight. Zafar Mahal was encroached from all sides by unsightly new construction, squatters sat in its entrance hallway, scratchings of the initials of modern lovers visible on its ancient walls, and cricket being played in its front yard where elephants once trod, carrying royal cavalcades.

One day, I went out in search of the tomb of Razia Sultan, the first female Muslim ruler of the subcontinent, who sat on the throne of Delhi in the 13th century. I had read about it previously and Google showed its location near the Turkman Gate of Old Delhi. On the way, I saw offices of a few travel agencies offering Hajj and Umrah packages, a large logo of Hamdard Dawakhana and the small decrepit dargah of Shah Turkman Bayabani under the shadow of the much larger gate that was named after him. The route I wanted to follow to reach Razia Sultan's tomb seemed to be blocked with construction. I asked a couple of people who had no clue of its whereabouts.

Inadvertently, I ended up inside a primary school. The murals on the walls of the school building were so captivating that I forgot about my quest and started contemplating the painted images of various yoga asanas, traditional dances from various Indian states, maps of those states, illustrations warning about the hazards of global warming, quotations on the importance of education and slogans for female literacy.

HUBH
AXMI

6

The Newer Ways of New Delhi

DRIVING ON THE ROAD THAT IS VARIOUSLY KNOWN BY THE FAMILIAR names of Grand Trunk Road or The Mall, I passed by a neighbourhood called Khyber Pass on my right and a mosque called Pathan Wali Masjid to my left. Not a single day passed in Delhi without me noticing a sign or building that connected me back home. Once, when traveling in a cab with Shivam Vij, a journalist friend based in Delhi, he pointed in the direction of Delhi's prestigious educational institution, St. Stephen's College.

"Do you know which prominent Pakistani's alma mater this is?" he asked.

I was ignorant on the subject.

"General Zia-ul-Haq," he answered his own question. General Zia-ul-Haq was the military dictator who ruled Pakistan from 1977 to 1988.

The few Delhiite friends that I had known through social media for years, and some of whom I only got to meet in person upon my arrival in India, took me around the famous hangout spots of the city during the evenings. One such place was the famous Khan Market. This market is named after Khan Abdul Jabbar Khan, also known as Dr. Khan Sahib, who was the chief minister of the province that I hail from, i.e. the North-West Frontier Province (which was renamed 'Khyber-Pakhtunkhwa' to represent its cultural and ethnic character rather than its geography in relation to the rest of India, and subsequently Pakistan, more than a century after being established as a province during British rule). Dr. Khan Sahib was also the elder brother of the legendary Pashtun leader and proponent of nonviolent resistance against the British colonial rule, Khan Abdul Ghaffar Khan, also known as Bacha Khan. The market was thus named by Hindu traders who had migrated from the North-West Frontier Province to honour Dr. Khan Sahib's efforts in helping them migrate to India safely during the riots of Partition. The market today is a bustling hub with many fancy cafés and high-end stores. We had kebab rolls from Khan Chacha at Khan Market.

Shivam and Arunav took me to the gentrified Hauz Khas Village named after a large water reservoir built during the times of the Delhi Sultanate. Sitting in a rooftop bar overlooking the pond, cooled by a large pedestal fan, we devoured the rather intriguing fusion invention of gulab jaman cheesecake while songs from Pakistani Coke Studio played in the background.

At Connaught Place, Shivam introduced me to his friend, Arpan Chaudhry, who was keen to talk about the place in Pakistan, not far from my hometown, where his great grandparents had migrated from. We met at United Coffee House, an eight decades-old restaurant featuring opulent colonial décor. Outside, a colossal Tricolour was hoisted on a towering pole. Several stray dogs rested indifferently in the middle of the shaded corridors of Connaught Place, where human traffic was always heavy. I kept worrying that their tails would get trampled upon by a distracted passer-by.

In Mehrauli, I walked from Khawaja Bakhtiyar Kaki's dargah to meet Arunav and his friend, the writer Farah Bashir, at a very tastefully decorated restaurant, serving Armenian cuisine. Who would have thought of finding an Armenian restaurant in Delhi! On its rooftop terrace, we had dinner and then sat for hours in swing sofas, chatting away, as I was once again overcome with wonder at the fact that my dream of visiting India and hanging out with my friends there had become a reality.

A friend suggested that when I go to Nizamuddin dargah, I must try the beef kebabs sold in a nearby lane. I was in disbelief that beef kebabs could be sold out in the open in the current times, after having heard of the fatal consequences of such dangerous pursuits. Cows are considered sacred in Hinduism and reports of vigilante violence against people suspected of carrying or selling cow meat had been in the news often. It turned out that the kebabs were in fact made from *buff,* a term used for buffalo meat. I recalled having heard the same term a few years ago during my visit to Nepal. I noted it as a welcome addition to the rich and expanding vocabulary of Indian English, which also has its own peculiar uses and variations of common English words. The kebabs were scrumptious, albeit quite fatty.

Prem Kumar came all the way from Bhubaneshwar to spend a day with me in Delhi. We had met in Lagos, Nigeria, several years ago, where he had become a great friend and my guide to the crowded metropolis. I mention it here because it was he who took me to the Indian Independence Day celebration at the Consulate of India in Lagos on 15th August 2010, where I tried to sing "*Jana Gana Mana*" along with everyone else and learned, after many attempts, the tongue-twister name for Independence Day in Hindi, i.e. *Swatantrata Devas*! During our meeting in Delhi, we went to eat at the charmingly named 'Oh! Calcutta' to try some delectable offerings of Bengali cooking.

In Delhi, the overall condition of roads, buildings, traffic, shops and neighbourhoods did not look markedly different from the cities of Pakistan. The quality (or lack thereof) of municipal services was arguably on par, if not worse, than Pakistani cities. Take out the ubiquitous signs in Hindi, and one could be forgiven for thinking one is roaming the streets of Pakistan rather than Delhi. But just then, a cycle rickshaw appears to remind you where you are, since this mode of transport has disappeared from Pakistani roads. On that count too, my city Dera Ismail Khan was the last one in Pakistan to discontinue the use of cycle rickshaws in 1991–92. These rickshaws reminded me of the many rides we had taken in those days, mostly for a fare of less than Rs. 5 in the 1980s.

The real contrast was in the state of India's air traffic. Indira Gandhi International Airport was busier than the top 10 busiest airports of Pakistan combined. Additionally, hotels of every star denomination in Delhi far outnumbered those in any city of Pakistan, which was a testament to the level of economic activity and flow of tourists and visitors from inside and outside the country.

Delhi's underground metro system is world-class, with an extensive network, spotless stations and efficiently running trains. Some Delhiites asked me, with obvious pride in their tone, what I thought of their metro network. They could be rightly proud of it, I would respond. The sign warning passengers at every metro station, "Caution: You are under surveillance" shows a pair of such sensuous eyes, that one is bound to drop any objections to being surveilled.

On the roads, one can't help but admire the progress made by India's automobile sector, seeing all the locally produced makes of vehicles. The vast majority of two- and three-wheelers are India's local brands, like Bajaj, TVS, Hero, etc. Most of the small- and medium-sized cars are manufactured in India, either by India's home-grown manufacturers or by international companies, but tailored to the Indian market.

I was disappointed to note, however, that the iconic Hindustan Motors Ambassador, the symbol of Indian auto industry's self-reliance, had all but disappeared from the roads. It was the car I was used to seeing in Bollywood films, out of which would emerge important men in white suits, trailed by the exaggerated but pleasing sound of their footsteps on hard, shiny floors. It also used to be cited as an example of the austerity practised by the Indian government and its disdain for imported luxury goods, in contrast to Pakistan, where anyone and everyone in high office felt entitled to a fleet of imported bulletproof German cars.

Early one morning on my return from Jaipur, the train passed through slums that stretched for miles on both sides of the track. I saw a man with his bare behind squatting by the side to defecate, completely unperturbed by the approaching train. Relieving oneself in full view of everyone did not seem to be out of the ordinary, since no one seemed to take special notice. When I reached Delhi and exited the station, I tried to avoid the crowd of taxi and auto drivers looking for custom and walked into a side street. The street was almost deserted, but I found a lonely auto parked on one side.

As I got closer, I called out to ask if the auto was free for a ride. The driver, who had been dozing in his seat, sat up, startled. He lazily agreed to take me to my hotel for a fare, that I found surprisingly low, considering the distance. He must have been running short of luck that day, because as he was meandering through the traffic, a traffic warden asked him to stop near a signal. He was hit with a fine equal to double the amount of my trip fare. With a stammer in his voice, he asked the cop what he had done wrong.

"*Bohat badhiya* (very nice), you want to know your fault, eh? I will pass on to you a word of wisdom: Do not ask me about your fault! Because, if I start counting the number of violations you have committed, your fine will be ten times more. Firstly, you are not wearing the uniform; second, your windshield has a crack in it; third, your indicator is not in the right place..." the uniformed warden went on.

The poor auto driver realised his tenuous position and said imploringly, "Okay, okay, sir, no problem, thank you. I will pay the fine, sir."

He got back into the auto and to my disbelief, praised the traffic warden in his stammering voice for what he deemed kind treatment.

"After all, they are just doing their duty. They stand there all day, dealing with thousands of people. If you are rude to them, they will obviously get angry at you. They are also humans like us, not *janaawar* (animal)," he explained.

I paid him the fare and a tip to cover the fine and reflected not only on his worldview but also about the peculiar way in which he pronounced the word for animal. It was unlike the standard Hindi diction and reminded me of the way it is pronounced in my native Pashto.

Despite the deepening communal fault lines due to the resurgence of Hindutva nationalism, it was possible to enter a church, a mosque, a gurudwara and a mandir without being asked to prove one's faith or identity. My solo walking tour took me from Sri Bangla Sahib Gurudwara to Sacred Heart Cathedral to Sri Laxmi Narayan Mandir. En route, I passed by a Sufi shrine, a Shia mosque and a Jain temple, all within the radius of about one mile. This commingling of faiths, even if only demonstrated in the geographical proximity of their real estate, was breathtaking. At none of those places was I stopped and asked to disclose my faith, though at the mandir I was a bit nervous thinking what I would say if someone asked. Pretending to be a local was not something I had practised and perfected yet. Yet, while walking towards the mandir, when a passerby stopped me to ask the directions to a government office, that by sheer chance I had seen earlier, I felt quite self-satisfied at my ability to direct a local inhabitant to an address in his own city.

It was very different to how things have come to pass in Pakistan, where space for representation of minority faiths has continued to shrink. On the other hand, recent reports from India indicate that it is following a similar path and losing its inclusive character, for which it was the envy of those holding secular ideals dear.

बेटी बचाओ
बेटी पढ़ाओ
علم ایک روشنی ہے
विद्या
विद्या
पीकर
विद्या
बहुत
विद्या एक
विद्या

Calvin Klein

7

Qutub and Farid Came in the Wedding Procession

THE MYSTICAL ATMOSPHERE AT EACH OF THE DARGAHS I VISITED IS probably the norm there all year round, but its effect was accentuated during the holy month of Ramzaan. Visiting these shrine complexes provided a glimpse into a syncretic, inclusive sub-culture that has developed over centuries. Its roots are in the Islamic teachings that arrived with the first Muslim conquerors, but incorporates various other ingredients derived from older indigenous faiths.

Walking towards the shrine of Hazrat Nizamuddin Auliya, which lends its name to the whole neighbourhood, I passed through narrow covered streets lined with shops selling rose petals and jasmine garlands, *chadars* (ceremonial cloth printed with Quranic verses for spreading on the shrine as an offering), *tasbeehs* (prayer beads), prayer mats, *ittar* (perfumed oils), stone-studded rings and prayer books.

In some of those shops, I saw a booklet titled "*Pakistani Panjsurah*". The peculiar name caught my eye. *Panj* means five and *surah* means a chapter of the Holy Quran. Hence *Panjsurah* refers to the compilation of five Quranic chapters that are considered auspicious. This uniquely South Asian compilation is sold in Pakistan as well, but without the national prefix in its title. I wondered what could have led to the naming of this compilation after Pakistan in India only, but my search on the topic did not point me to any leads about its origins.

Among other books prominently displayed at those shops were titles in Hindi such as "*Auliya-e-Hind-o-Pak*" (Sufi saints of India and Pakistan), "*Aadaab-e-Mubaashirat – mian-biwi ke sharirik sambandh ka Islami tareeqa*" (Etiquette of Sex – the Islamic way of carnal relations between husband and wife) and "*Taskheer-e-Jinnaat*" (Conquering the Djinns). There were a few titles in Urdu and Bengali as well. The breadth of topics covered by the religious literature on offer was notable.

The sound of qawwali that I could hear before entering the dargah made me quicken my steps. The melodious music got louder as I got nearer. Inside, a group of qawwals was assembled outside the shrine, singing the qawwali, surrounded by listeners sitting on the ground. Men wore skull caps and women covered their heads with dupattas. There were no separate sections for the two genders.

Fans hanging from poles whirred, the marble floors had cooled down after the hot day, the whole area was lit with festive lights, the air was serene. I lined up to enter the structure that housed the actual tomb of Hazrat Nizamuddin Auliya. Its dome was covered in electric lights. There was a sign outside that read "Ladies are not allowed in side (sic)". Gender equality had reached a dead end. Even at Sufi shrines, considered bastions of love for all beings, certain aspects of patriarchy prevailed.

The ladies, who were not allowed to enter the tomb, tied threads to its latticed stone windows and peeked in from outside. The men, who were allowed inside, stood respectfully around the grave, covered with *chaadars* and rose petals, their heads bowed and their palms raised in prayer.

Another room in the complex housed the tomb of Hazrat Nizamuddin Auliya's most favourite disciple, the mystic poet-musician, Amir Khusrau, who wrote many verses in romantic devotion to his beloved spiritual master. One of his famous couplets is:

Qutub Farid mil aaye baraati
Khursau raajdulari Nijaam
"Qutub and Farid have come in the wedding party
And Khursau is the loving bride of Nizam"

Qutub and Farid refer to the Sufi saints Khawaja Qutubuddin Bakhtiyar Kaki (buried in Mehrauli, Delhi) and Fariduddin Ganj-i-Shakar (buried in Pakpattan, Pakistan), who preceded Nizam in the Chishti Sufi order.

Upon leaving Amir Khusrau's shrine, I noticed an Urdu plaque with Allama Iqbal's name on it. It had lines from a qawwali that he was mesmerised by when he heard it at the dargah.

Hind ka daata hai tu, tera bara darbaar hai
Kuch mile ham ko bhi is darbaar-e-gohar baar se
(You are the benefactor of India, your court is grand
Bestow something from this treasure-filled court on me too)

Khawaja Qutubuddin Bakhtiyar Kaki (mentioned in Amir Khusrau's couplet above) is the other very important Sufi saint buried in Delhi. His dargah is situated a long distance away from Nizamuddin in the neighbourhood of Mehrauli. I visited the dargah the day I visited Qutub Minar. The similarity in the name of the tower and the eternally resting resident of the shrine was only coincidental, as they were two different Qutubs – one a Sultan of Delhi and the other a mystic and Sufi. However, some say that it's possible the minaret is named after the Sufi. Who knows? The sultans were often committed devotees of the saints as well and attributed their conquests to holy blessings.

After observing the lamentable state of Zafar Mahal, a palatial building from the later Mughal era, situated outside, I approached the dargah complex. A woman coming out noticed me, as I was going in. I was carrying an Urdu magazine I had bought earlier that day in the same hand in which I held my shoes that I had just taken off.

She called out, *"Bhai, siparah aur joote ek hi haath mein uttha rakhe hain, kucch toh rehm karo."* (Brother, you are carrying the *siparah* (a volume of Quran) and your shoes in the same hand! Please have some mercy.)

I showed her the book and said, "Sister, it's not a *siparah*, but a magazine of Urdu poetry."

"Oh accha, phir theek hai. Maaf karna, bhai." (Oh okay, that's all right then. Forgive me, brother).

A few minutes remained till the setting of the sun. I was walking around, going from grave to grave inside the shrine complex, trying to read their inscriptions. An elderly man, sitting by a grave, observed me with interest. I said salaam to him.

"*Kashmiri ho*?" he asked me.

"*Nahin, Pakistan se aaya hoon* (No, I have come from Pakistan)."

***

People started sitting in rows in preparation for the iftar meal that was about to be served. Old newspapers served as trays, in which dates, pakoras, jalebis and samosas were being dropped by volunteers walking around.

The gates to the enclosure housing the graves of the Khawaja and his closest associates had been shut before maghrib prayers. The wall of the entrance had a lot of little niches for oil lamps. I had iftar at the shrine along with the faithfuls of Mehrauli and then headed to the graves. A Persian couplet of Mevlana Rumi was inscribed on top of the doorway:

Kaaba-tul ushaaq baashud een maqam
Har keh naaqis aamad een baashud tamaam
(This place holds the status of Kaaba for lovers of its occupant
They come with their faults and leave after attaining perfection)

As the gathering waited for the enclosure to be reopened, a man prostrated at the door full of floral carvings. Outside, a sign prohibited the entry of "females and girls". Inside, a massive chandelier hung over the Khawaja's expansive grave from the beautifully decorated ceiling. Devotees walked backwards when leaving, so as to avoid turning their back to the grave.

As I was on my way out, a group of qawwals sat in the courtyard began striking the initial notes of a qawwali in their coarsely melodious voices. I stopped in my tracks. I had to join friends for dinner but could not tear myself away from the spell that was being cast. I sat on the marble floor. The lead qawwal nodded in my direction. I turned my phone to silent and listened intently with my eyes closed. What are friends for, if not to wait a little longer for you, when you're trapped in compelling situations?

8

Widows, Bulls, Stairs and Ascetics

THE HEAT WAS RELENTLESS IN VARANASI, THE NEW NAME OF THE CITY that one had heard of as Benaras in songs and stories. Apparently, the new name is older than the city's old name that has simply been restored; such is the intermesh of old and new in India's history. When it is explored and revised to separate the native from the foreign, one realises that the lines separating them are very murky. The city has an even older name, Kashi, and it does not take long to realise that somehow all the names of the city are still in currency.

When I handed my passport to the Muslim receptionist at the hotel, he told me with a glint in his eye that his aunt lived in Karachi. The language he spoke sounded very refined and polite, sprinkled with *keejiye, leejiye, deejiye*. I experienced the same refined tone everywhere in Benaras.

I had started feeling the effect of unseasonal cold and fever. Roaming around the city, I realised I could not wish it away and went to a pharmacy. Fortunately (or unfortunately, depending on the situation one finds oneself in) just like in Pakistan, it is possible to get antibiotics over the counter in India. While GPs in England always warn against the risks of resorting to antibiotics to treat viral infections, somehow, they proved to be very effective in putting a South Asian man back on his feet in a single day. Therefore, I trusted the prescription of the pharmacist and it worked.

Benaras was overloaded with mystical charm. All the winding lanes of the old city led to various *ghats* by the river Ganges (Ganga). Each *ghat* was made of riverfront steps and associated buildings for performing ritual baths and worship. Earlier in Delhi, an old virtual friend and author, Veejay Sai, came to see me and shared with me the famous lines of 15th century mystic poet, Kabir, about the city:

Raand, saand, seerhi, sanyasi, in se bache to seve kasi

(Widows, bulls, stairs and ascetics / Escape them all to reach salvation [Kashi – the old name of the city, which also means salvation])

The city proved true to this reputation, as upon approaching the *ghats*, one finds countless stairs leading down to the river.

Homeless widows can be seen sitting in the corridors and passageways, identified by their white saris and occasionally shaved heads. Bulls sit or walk with their royal gait, at times not leaving any room for pedestrians to pass by in narrow lanes. Ascetics with long hair, painted white lines on their foreheads, and nothing covering their body except a loincloth, are a ubiquitous sight.

Here, every building seemed to hold the history of countless human lives over numerous generations. Lives of ordinary men and women, not of royal personages. The low doorways of houses in the streets, framed by carved panels and alcoves on either side, seemed to be leading into secret chambers, where domestic intrigues were still being played out. Many houses had figures of Hindu deities painted on top of the entrance. Some had profiles of what looked like turbaned guards holding swords painted on both sides of the entrance. Women in saris sat by the roadside selling vegetables. Garbage was scattered everywhere. A banner outside a school building read: "Admission Open: *Aao khel khel mein parhna seekhein* (Let's learn to read while playing)." The city had an enchanted air. I was captivated right away.

Benaras is also a city where people go to die. There are designated establishments in the city which cater to the old and infirm only, who go there to await death and thus attain "salvation". One walks around the city and observes the faces of people, wondering who among them are resigned to die and who are living to keep the venture of death running. In the narrow streets, one must step aside from time to time to make way for the bodies of the dead, being carried away hastily by men towards the *ghats*. I used to look closely at their faces to find signs of grief or mourning, but in Benaras, death is unremarkable.

Summer afternoons at the *ghats* were rather quiet. Some people took their siestas on hard floors and in the large doorways of the buildings around the ghats. The glistening skin of their shirtless bodies appeared thoroughly sunburned. I was impressed by the dexterity of the cows, as they effortlessly climbed up and down the steps of the *ghats*. One woman fed white sliced bread to a cow from a packet that I had seen her buying from a shop earlier. The domes and minarets of an imposing mosque were visible in the distance among the row of ghats. Dogs roamed around or rested on the steps. Groups of boys played cricket with the uneven *ghats* as their pitch. At one *ghat* I stopped to observe a cremation. The smell of burning meat permeated the air. One arm of the corpse slowly stuck out as the rest of it burned, making crackling sounds.

The message written on the walls at several places remained completely unheeded, *"Kripya ghaton par gandgi na karein"* (Please don't litter at the *ghats*). At one of the ghats, a sketch of what looked like several devotees sitting respectfully in front of a saint with a halo around his head, was engraved on the wall accompanied by the text, *"Jaati paati puchhe nahin koi, Hari bhaje so Hari ka hoye"* (Nobody should inquire about caste – whoever worships God belongs to God).

Walking further, I found a young woman in a rather dishevelled condition sitting on the steps. She was barefoot and wore a kurta over jeans. Burn marks were visible on her face. A man gave her a bottle of cold water, as she recounted her ordeal incoherently. Perhaps she had been mistreated by her family or her in-laws. A serious-looking man listened to her sceptically and interjected from time to time,

"Sach bol rahi ho na?" (Are you really telling the truth?)

Looking at her pitiable state, and finally assured of her honesty, he then asked her,

"Baba ke darshan karna chahti ho?" (Do you want to visit/pay respects to the Baba?)

He was alluding to a visit to one of the holiest Hindu temples in Benaras, Kashi Vishwanath Mandir, or to Lord Shiva, to whom it is dedicated. I walked on.

9

Escape Them All to Find Salvation

IN THE EVENING, I TOOK A RIDE IN ONE OF THE MANY BOATS WAITING for passengers on the Ganges. From the boat floating on the waves of the river Ganges, one can have spectacular views of the bank and the long row of *ghats* hugging it. It is said that there are 84 ghats in Benaras. From some of them, I could see smoke emitting from funeral pyres.

The holy water of Ganges looks forbiddingly dirty, but that does not prevent people, who come from near and far, to take a dip and have their sins washed away. Birds hover over the water and sometimes descend to pick at items floating on the surface. I wondered if those floating items, visible in the distance, were pieces of garbage, or remains of bodies not fully burned.

The cawing of crows grew louder as the sun was setting. Lights began flickering from the ghats and were reflected in the water. The faint sound of faraway bells could also be heard, but I could not tell if it was coming from a temple on the riverbank or from deep inside the riverbed of the Ganges, which must have been covered with layers upon layers of ash particles, blending the fresh and ancient together in a never-ending march towards oblivion.

At dusk, an impressive ceremony takes place on the *ghats*. It's called Ganga Aarti, meaning Prayer for the River Ganges. The ceremony comprises hymn-singing and the performance of rituals that are a sight to behold from the boat. A group of young pandits wave and circle large burning lamps in elaborate synchronised patterns. The air is smoky and filled with the scent of burning oil and wood. Lights emitted from lamps compete with lights from smartphone screens.

I find it mindboggling that a city like Benaras, oozing with history and mystery, has not yet been designated as a UNESCO World Heritage Site. I have visited cities in other parts of the world that are not a patch on Benaras in terms of historical significance and architectural value, yet they have been given that recognition. Negligence towards the preservation of heritage is perhaps another common South Asian trait. But in a place where millions of people are not sure about getting their two daily meals, preservation of heritage cannot sit at the top of the priority list.

Arunav joined me again in Benaras. We went to a traditional restaurant we were recommended, called Baati Chokha. The food served was very different from the common North Indian fare I was familiar with. What delighted me the most was the salty lassi-like drink on the menu called *mattha*. It was the first time I had heard this word outside my hometown, Dera Ismail Khan, where it is used for a raita-like side accompanying the traditional *sobat* dish (a communal meal prepared by soaking pieces of torn flatbread in a meat or chicken broth). Both of these items originate from yoghurt, which explains why they are known by the same name but have evolved slightly differently in use.

Kachoris (a deep-fried stuffed pastry with savoury fillings) served in disposable bowls made of natural leaf are very commonly served at roadside food stalls in Benaras and Delhi. I ate kachoris with abandon and drank more cups of chai out of earthen cups in Benaras than I care to remember, but not at the expense of cool sweet lassi. In Pakistan, samosas enjoy a lot more prominence than kachoris and bowls made of leaf have not come to my notice yet.

Talking of chai, a friend from Delhi had recommended that I make a stop at Pappu's Tea Stall. The chai shop is situated close to Assi Ghat. I had already wanted to visit Assi Ghat, as it features in the title of a Hindi novel *Kashi ka Assi* by Kashinath Singh, recommended to me by Shilpi Gulati with a warning about its expletive-laden language, when she learned that I was going to visit Benaras.

Pappu's Tea Stall is famous for the political debates that take place there, similar to the debates and conversations found in the novel *Kashi ka Assi*. It is a very unassuming place with no signboard outside. I was disappointed, however, to find it closed. Inquiry at the shop next door revealed that the store was closed because "*Un ke bhai guzar gaye*" (Pappu's brother had passed away).

On the way back, I noticed a clothing shop called 'Multani & Sons', with an 'Eid Mubarak' banner hung over its entrance. It was offering discounts on kurta pajamas. They were expecting to do good business in anticipation of the upcoming Eid. At the centre of a traffic square, a statue of holy mother cow sat atop a pedestal, while the mad traffic below negotiated its way under her watchful eye. A girl riding a scooter stopped nearby due to the jammed traffic. Our eyes interlocked for a few seconds. The traffic congestion eased, and she whizzed away. My heartbeat also eased.

Learning about the entry restrictions placed on non-Hindus to the most important temple in Benaras, the Kashi Vishwanath Mandir, was a setback that I was reluctant to accept. What was astounding, however, was the presence of a mosque adjacent to the temple. That historic and active place of worship, called Gyanvapi Mosque, was built by Mughal emperor Aurangzeb, likely on the site of a demolished Hindu temple. The location and history of the mosque make it a very sensitive site. The atmosphere seemed charged, with heavy police presence.

The narrow streets leading to the temple area were filled with people queuing up for *darshan* (viewing or paying respects) and seeking blessings. Men in shops on both sides of the street were offering foodstuff to be taken as *prasad* (offering) to the temple and depositing shoes of the pilgrims for safekeeping. An elderly woman sat on the ground, threading marigold flowers into garlands.

I thought I could pass off as a local and join the queues, but the eyes of the shop owners on both sides, trained to spot non-locals, would rest on me with suspicion. One of them addressed me in English, asking me if I needed a guide. Another one warned me that foreigners were not allowed inside the temple. When I surprised one of them by responding in Urdu/Hindi and pretending to be an Indian, he said in an ingratiating tone,

"Aap ki look ed dam bidesi hai." (You appear just like a foreigner).

"Ek dam superstar lagte ho," (You look like a filmstar) the man behind me in the queue remarked.

Several people giggled. Though flattering, I could hardly welcome such attention in that situation. I kept slowly trudging along in the queue leading to the temple with nervousness, thinking I ought not to be there. The eyes of Yogi Adityanath, the populist firebrand chief minister of the state, were watching me from the posters splashed on the walls.

I stopped at a shop to leave my shoes there. The shopkeeper asked me if I needed to take *prasad* with me to the temple. Out of sheer naivete, I made the faux pas of asking the price of *prasad*. He smiled and understood that I was completely uninitiated. He offered that a pandit guide could accompany me into the temple. But I could see signs on the walls saying clearly, "Only Hindus allowed." Sensing my hesitation, he asked,

"Hindu toh ho na bhai?" (You are a Hindu, right?)

At that moment, I thought to myself that the eternal message of all belief systems invited mankind to the same set of virtues, so regardless of whichever faith's adherent I pass myself as, why it should make any difference. Before I could answer, the man from the *prasad* shop shot another question my way, asking where I was from.

"Kashmir," I said hesitatingly, not realising I was getting myself deeper into trouble. The young pandit guide dragged me by my arm into the queue and said, *"Koi poochhe to Jambu* (sic) *Kashmir bol dena."* (If someone asks, just say you are from Jambu (sic) Kashmir)

After a tour of the complex, I was brought before the senior pandit for an interview. My heart was pounding hard. The senior pandit told me to sit down and repeat the chanting after him. He started a long prayer in completely unrecognisable Sanskrit, and I repeated every sentence after him. Whether those were words of praise for Lord Shiva or prayers for my deliverance, I don't know, but in the middle of the chant, he stopped to ask me a few questions in Hindi, like:

"Naam kya hai?" (What's your name?)

"Maata pita jeevat hain?" (Are your parents alive?)

"Service karte ho ya beopaar?" (Are you in employment or do you have your own business?)

I believe he was tailoring the Sanskrit prayer based on my answers, most of which were true, apart from a few. At long last the prayer ended, and I was asked to make a donation. That donation turned out to be the heftiest expense of my entire India trip, but I felt it was money well spent.

Incidents of lynching of Muslims on allegations of carrying beef or transporting cows were being reported in the media while I was there. In that context, my presence as a Pakistani in the streets of one of the holiest Indian cities at a place demarcated for Hindus only, made me, in the words of an Indian Muslim friend, the perfect candidate for lynching. That is why I heaved a massive sigh of relief when I emerged safely from the adventure, with a *tilak* on my forehead.

I headed back towards the Ganges, as its lure was too strong, and the stories played out on the steps of its ghats were never-ending. In the street, I saw a bright, green-coloured kiosk raised on wooden legs. Inside sat a middle-aged woman selling saris. As she noticed me taking a photo of the view of which she was a part, an endearingly shy expression appeared on her face, as she fixed the side of her scarf over her head to appear more presentable for the camera. I reached a *ghat* where pieces of wood were being laid over a dead body to prepare it for cremation. The whole body was covered, but the face was left exposed. As oil was sprinkled over the pyre and the fire was lit, people attending the funeral gathered around and observed in a manner that seemed very nonchalant to me. Were they the relatives of the deceased? If so, why did they appear so unaffected? Why was there no mournful crying and tragic wailing at any of the funerals? In Benaras, death was very matter-of-fact, a mere transition from being to nothingness.

After making sure I witnessed the cremation until the end, I walked onwards to the next *ghat*, which presented a striking view of colourful saris spread out on the steps for drying. They likely belonged to the women who had just taken a dip in the Ganges. Amongst the hundreds of bulls and cows roaming around leisurely in every part of the city, there was one resting nearby, in a very convoluted pose that made me worry about the condition of its health. A few steps ahead, a couple of roadside barbers were shaving off the heads of men, young and old. I learned that it is a Hindu custom for men to shave their heads in Benaras, as a way of inculcating humility and getting closer to God. It has an amazing similarity to the Islamic ritual of shaving the head at the conclusion of Hajj and Umrah rituals.

10

Through the Heart of Uttar Pradesh

Traveling from Benaras to Agra in a sleeper bus was an experience that can perhaps only be had in India. Nowhere else had I seen a bus from which all the seats had been removed, to be replaced with a double layer of sleeping berths. For good purpose.

Sitting in the bus, browsing through news stories on my phone, I came across a report by Uttar Pradesh (UP) government that domestic tourist preferred Varanasi over Taj Mahal. There was a statement from UP's chief minister that the minarets of Taj Mahal did not represent Indian culture, therefore the practice of gifting replicas of Taj Mahal to foreign dignitaries was going to be discontinued. To replace that, copies of *Gita* would be given as presents. I showed the stories to my fellow passenger. A frown appeared on his face as he shook his head, suggesting I should refrain from bringing up such unpleasant topics in conversation. It was another indication of gradual shunning of vital aspects of India's rich cultural heritage by its officialdom and thus stripping it of its inclusive character.

The hotel in Agra where I had booked a room sent an email declining to host me after noticing that I was from Pakistan. I did not blame them; the paperwork required for hosting Pakistanis was quite a hassle and perhaps not worth the room rent they could have earned from me.

I found another hotel to stay at. After check-in, I went to have tea at a roadside café, where I started talking to other customers. Not knowing where I had come from, one of them discouraged me from visiting the Taj Mahal.

"Taj Mahal is nothing. Go to Mathura, go to Vrindavan, to see what beauty actually looks like."

Needless to say, I ignored his advice and arrived at the Taj at midday. Without the slightest touch of hyperbole, I can say that words cannot capture the splendour of Taj Mahal. It truly is unmatchable in every sense of the word. The conception and execution of such a monument is a testament to the amazing ability of humans to work miracles. The kind of perfection it embodies cannot be imagined today, let alone executed.

The Taj is flanked by two identical buildings on each side, one of which is a functional mosque and the other used to serve as a guest house for royal visitors.

When I visited, restoration work was ongoing, revealing how much the marble on the dome and minarets had yellowed. The scaffolding on two of the minarets were an eyesore, but the magnificence of the building compelled me to stay and admire it from every angle for as long as I could.

The Taj Mahal is not the only important site from the Mughal era in Agra. There are several others worth a visit. The sprawling Agra Fort is almost the size of a small city. It used to serve as the main residence of Mughal rulers before they shifted the capital to Delhi. In one of the rooms of the fort, I heard a tour guide telling his group that emperor Shah Jahan was incarcerated in that room for 8 years by his son, Aurangzeb. It was a beautiful marble room, intricately decorated with patterns of inlaid gems. Shah Jahan used to look at the Taj Mahal he had built as his beloved wife's final resting place from the window of that room.

As I exited the Agra Fort, I saw a group of women appearing somewhat lost. They were clothed in fitted shalwar-kameez. I wondered which state they might have come from – Punjab, Haryana, Rajasthan? One of them approached me to ask if I had been inside the fort. I answered in the affirmative. She asked if I had taken any photos. I nodded. She demanded that I show them the photos. I took out my phone and started swiping the photos on the screen before this group of three women. They looked at the photos with intense concentration, letting out occasional gasps of wonder. The older one among the women said, "*Chalo bhai, dekh liya.*" (That's it, we've seen it).

They turned back from the road leading to the fort's entrance. It took me a few moments to realise that they could not afford the 40-rupee ticket to enter the fort, despite their evident desire to see the inside of it. It struck me that the passion for sightseeing was not something that could be fulfilled without a degree of privilege.

***

Early next morning, I went to Mehtab Bagh, a garden complex to the north of Taj Mahal that offers breathtaking views of the Taj without any hordes and hubbub. The tomb of Itimad-ud-Daulah was my next stop, which was a delight in its own right. I was ignorant of its existence at the time of planning my trip to Agra. The architectural style of Itimad-ud-Daulah's tomb is very unique among all the Mughal monuments, as it does not feature a dome. The motifs of aesthetic floral patterns, made with studded precious stones, were mostly intact. Light entered through delicately perforated stone windows. Quiet and surrounded by gardens, it was a serene place that morning.

Just outside Agra is the old Mughal capital Fatehpur Sikri that was built by emperor Akbar the Great. Here, the single best decision I made was to rent an audio guide. The style and effect of its storytelling was exquisite. I wished I had taken audio guides at other forts, palaces and mosques I had visited earlier, but at least I thoroughly enjoyed the one at Fatehpur Sikri.

The complex of Fatehpur Sikri is just one more of the many magnificent remnants from the era of Mughal rule. Its architectural style has a strong domestic Indian flavour and is mostly built in red sandstone. The complex includes the Jama Masjid which houses the tomb of the Sufi saint, Salim Chishti. Salim Chishti's devotees included emperor Akbar himself, who named his son Salim in honour of the saint. It was the same Shahzada Salim who went on to become emperor Jahangir and continues to be portrayed as a lead character in many films and novels to this day due to his legendary love affair with Anarkali.

Even though I reached the Jama Masjid of Fatehpur Sikri in the afternoon when the sun was right overhead, a group of qawwals were already sitting outside the shrine on the marble floor of the courtyard, singing to enthral the visitors.

I realised that I had reached the end of the time allotted to me by my taxi driver to explore Fatehpur Sikri, so I headed out of the Jama Masjid. Before finding him, I found a group of pigs rummaging through garbage in the parking lot.

My next stop was Sikandra, a suburb of Agra, where the emperor who ordered the marvellous city of Fatehpur Sikri to be built is himself buried. Akbar's tomb is another very fine piece of architecture. The burial chamber is cool and dark with walls devoid of any decoration. The only light comes from the passage through which one enters. Curiously, in that dark room a group of men were asking for donations for a qawwali to be organised at the tomb. The group seemed to be of questionable legitimacy as Akbar's mausoleum, being neither the shrine of a holy saint nor a place of religious significance due to the emperor's secular credentials, was an unlikely site for organising a qawwali. My doubts intensified when the donation seekers started preventing visitors from taking photos of the tomb, though they were not part of the tomb's management.

An eatery in Agra that I chanced upon during my search for food turned out to be a noteworthy discovery. Named 'Sheroes Hangout', it was a café staffed entirely by survivors of acid attacks. It was sad to come face to face with another disgraceful similarity between India and Pakistan, for women in both countries have long been victims of this grotesque crime committed in the name of honour and revenge. It was encouraging, however, to see a venture dedicated to the rehabilitation of the survivors. There was no written price for any item on the menu. Customers were expected to pay what they deemed to be a fair price for their food and drink.

11

From Mughal Splendour to Rajput Grandeur

THE AUTO I HIRED ON MY SECOND DAY IN AGRA OUTSIDE MEHTAB Bagh was driven by a Muslim driver, who was quick to display solidarity upon learning where I was from. Before recommending restaurants for me to eat at, he asked, *"Ramzaan se ho?"* which I thought was a curious way of asking if I was fasting. He took me to a store selling *petha,* the famous sweet of Agra, where I was compelled to buy a few boxes. This turned out to be a mistake, because despite covering the boxes in plastic wrappers, the sticky syrup of *petha* seeped out to stain other contents of my suitcase.

On the way, our friendly and talkative auto driver also picked up other passengers, after sheepishly asking me if I would not mind. He announced to each one of them that I was from Pakistan, like he had done earlier at the *petha* shop, which resulted in some inquisitive stares directed at me. One of the passengers told me that his family had migrated from Lahore at the time of Partition.

Mention Pakistan and it does not take long for the conversation to turn to the subject of terrorism, which by an unfortunate extension, is linked to Indian Muslims as well. I cannot recall what turn the discussion took that made our auto driver proclaim "*Aatankwaad ka koi dharam nahin hota*" (Terrorism has no religion).

"Don't you remember what happened in the Samjhauta Express incident?" he asked of everyone present in his auto (which had the capacity for a maximum of two passengers, but was carrying five by that time), two of them half-sitting and half-hanging on either side of the driver.

"What happened?" I asked, genuinely unaware of the outcome of investigations into a bombing incident that targeted the only train running between India and Pakistan many years ago.

"The media, the politicians, the people, everyone blamed us Muslims for the bombings, like they do in every instance of terrorism, but the mastermind behind all of that turned out to be a Hindu nationalist, who was also involved in several bombings on mosques and dargahs in India," he replied.

"Really?" I exclaimed and looked around to see the expressions of other passengers who were squeezing me from all directions. Some of them seemed to have stopped listening over the din of the auto engine and the traffic, but the man whose family had migrated from Lahore looked thoroughly unconvinced.

"*Aur nahin tou kya*! Ask anybody about it," the auto driver added.

When it was time for my departure from Agra, I headed towards the Agra Cantt Railway Station. The auto driver reminded me a number of times that I must keep his mobile number saved and call him the next time I visited Agra. I nodded but wondered in my heart whether there would ever be a next time.

The station's name was displayed in white letters on a large blue background in Hindi and Urdu. The latter seemed to have been written by somebody who was probably a first-day student of Urdu *nastaliq* calligraphy.

Waiting for my train to Jaipur, I walked around and observed the goings-on around me. The ramp entrance for disabled people was supposedly destigmatized with the label "For differently abled passengers". A bookstall stocked many copies of the Hindi translation of the book *'I am Malala'* indicating it was a bestseller. Next to Malala's book, I saw another title *Mann ki Uljhanein kaise Suljhayen* (How to Resolve the Heart's Worries). Dogs freely roamed around. The stench of excrement floated in the air.

At a confectionary stall, I saw the price list and discovered that *petha* was sold there at less than half the price I had paid at the shop run by a Hindu man that my Muslim-solidarity auto driver had taken me to.

The announcements about train departures and platform numbers did not match the information on multiple display screens. I did not know which source to trust. A young provincial woman with a bare midriff and face fully covered in a semi-transparent *ghoonghat* walked past, swaying her hips. I wondered if she was also going to Jaipur, as my eyes followed her for as long as she was visible.

The day I made the train journey from Agra to Jaipur, Pakistan was playing against India in the final of the ICC Champions Trophy Cricket tournament. Cricket is taken very seriously in the subcontinent. Add the traditional rivalry of the two finalists to the mix, and you're in for one of the fiercest showdowns in sport. Despite temptation, I thought it best to keep my Pakistani identity under wraps, for a moving train is an enclosed space with little possibility of a safe escape.

The kids from the family sitting on the seats adjacent to mine started playing a quiz. One of them asked the other to name a place starting with A. "Amritsar", was the answer. The first one laughed and said that it reminded him of Amritsar. Perplexed as to what he meant by Amritsar reminding him of Amritsar, I started listening more attentively. It turned out he had a teacher at school by the name Amrit, and they used to call him "Amrit sir".

I closed my eyes to summon the image of the woman in *ghoonghat* I had seen at the Agra Cantt Railway Station. She was an enchanting sight amidst the stench of the station. Was she on the same train? Where was she from? Himachal? Rajasthan? UP? MP?

Awoken from my reverie by a noise on the train, I checked the progress of the match on my phone. The result was very satisfying. Pakistan had won the final! I looked around to see people's reactions, but everyone looked rather unconcerned. I was surprised with the apathy with which this cricket-loving nation handled its defeat. This would have been unimaginable in Pakistan, where any game of cricket lost to India results in a public outpouring of wrath against the national team and over-analysis of reasons for the defeat in the media as well as in the streets.

The next morning at the hotel, I received a copy of the *Hindustan Times* newspaper. The frontpage headline was, "India Trounce Pakistan 6-1 in Hockey". I turned the pages to find something about the cricket final from the day before. There was only a small single-column story on the last page about it. It was amusing to observe how hockey in India had all of a sudden risen from obscurity and surpassed cricket's popularity and importance.

The station near where I stayed in Jaipur was called Sindhi Camp. The man at the hotel reception gave me a somewhat cold welcome after I informed him of my nationality, but this was quickly compensated by the charm and homeliness of the single storey hotel building, surrounded by gardens and flowerbeds, separated by sawtooth brick edging. The bellhop, who was a Muslim, took the opportunity to give me a rundown of local restaurants serving halal fare.

He asked me if I intended to visit Ajmer, a city two hours away from Jaipur by road, famous for the dargah of Khawaja Moinuddin Chishti. I said I would have liked to, but my visa did not list Ajmer as a city I could visit. Perhaps I could go for a day trip, I asked him. He strongly advised me to not undertake such an adventure, as it could put me in trouble. "Times are not favourable," he added. I reluctantly put my desire to sleep and understood that I had not yet received a *bulawa* (invitation) to visit the dargah. As they say, no one can visit without one.

It was a bit late at night. I went out in search of food and felt a sense of familiarity in the nightly atmosphere of the streets. Little stores and unassuming cafés extending on to the sidewalks, plastic chairs laid out outside and groups of boys hanging about, some leaning against their parked motorcycles, some taking puffs of smoke and sips of chai. The language spoken in the streets of Rajasthan was the same that we identify as Hindi in India and Urdu in Pakistan.

12

The Fault in the Pink of Pink City

JAIPUR IS A CITY OF EYE-CATCHING PALACES. THEY WERE BUILT BY THE Rajput Maharajas of the former Jaipur princely state. There are so many of them that one is faced with the hard choice of which ones to visit and which ones to leave out. Jaipur is also nicknamed "the Pink City" because of the dominant colour scheme of its buildings. The shade looked less pink and more orange-ochre to me, however. I asked a taxi driver about this discrepancy between the shade and the name.

"Sir ji, woh colour mein thoda sa fault aa gaya hai" (The colour has become a bit faulty with time, sir), he explained, and I found his explanation completely faultless.

Some of the strikingly beautiful monuments that I saw in the city included the aberrantly named City Palace, the unique Hawa Mahal with its thousand windows, Jal Mahal in the middle of a lake (closed to visitors) and Jantar Mantar (not a palace), which is an open-air laboratory for astronomical observations and experiments. Most of these palaces and monuments presented a confluence of Rajput and Mughal styles of architecture. These palaces also had *Diwan-e-Khaas* and *Diwan-e-Aam* pavilions (halls for private and public audiences, respectively) that one finds in forts of the Mughal era. Images of peacocks feature prominently in the frescoes and carvings.

During a visit to one of the palaces, I overheard the fascinating tale of the title "Sawai" from a tour guide narrating it to his group. It was a title conferred on Maharaja Jai Singh II of Jaipur by the Mughal emperor Aurangzeb. According to the legend, when Jai Singh was a young prince of 11, he was taken by his father to pay a visit to emperor Aurangzeb's court in Delhi. Aurangzeb put his hand on the young prince's shoulder and asked him if he felt nervous. The young prince remained composed and responded that he saw no reason to feel scared when he was under the protection of the great emperor. Impressed by the confidence and intelligence of the young boy, Aurangzeb conferred on him the title of "Sawai", derived from the word *sawa,* meaning a quarter over one – in terms of intelligence in this case. The title became hereditary for Jai Singh's successors.

Later, when I recounted this story to a group of friends, the wittier amongst them extended the joke upon himself, saying if he was in place of the young prince, the emperor would have conferred the title of *pona* (a quarter less than one) on him.

Having explored the palaces within the city, my next stop was to go up the hill on the outskirts of the city to visit the Nahargarh Fort. I went there in the late afternoon to observe the sunset of the longest day of the year, which also happened to be my birthday. On the way to the fort, I passed by a neighbourhood named Karbala, after the holy Iraqi city of the same name.

The view of Jaipur from Nahargarh Fort is breathtaking, especially at sunset, as the sprawling city is lit up and the sounds of *azaan* from mosques and *bhajans* and *kirtans* from temples rise and intermingle in the air and echo through the mountains. I sat there on the rampart of the fort, watching the sun that had risen earlier that day go down, and with it sealing the addition of a number to my age. Arunav, who had arrived from Gurgaon earlier that day, had ordered a cake that we enjoyed while appreciating the spread of Jaipur from above.

The Jaigarh Fort and Amer Fort are also located in those hills. The palatial Amer Fort is another magnificent monument of Rajput architecture and a testament to the opulence enjoyed by the royals who built it. One of the main entrance portals, called Ganesh Pol, is a sight to behold, with its beautiful arches, latticed marble windows and intricate colourful frescoes. The palace also contains a dazzling chamber by the name of Sheesh Mahal (mirror palace), in keeping with the trend of such chambers found in several Mughal forts, apparently built with the intention of illuminating every hard-to-reach corner of the minds of visitors by reflecting every ray of light a million times.

I hailed a taxi every time I had to go somewhere. None of the taxi drivers missed the opportunity to tell me about the famous Hindi films filmed around those hills and palaces. Unnecessary honking by road users was very common in Jaipur. The incessant honking by one cab driver prompted me to suggest that he keep his hand pressed on the car's horn, so he could avoid the inconvenience of lifting and pressing alternatively. He did not look very impressed with my suggestion.

Back in the city from the hills, I found myself in a park near the Govind Devji Temple. A man was feeding sliced white bread from a packet to monkeys. I was reminded of the cow I had seen being fed by a woman near the *ghats* of Benaras. Sacred monkeys and sacred cows, symbols of gods of fertility, prosperity and power, are revered and fed by believers across India. I was tempted to tell the man to use wholemeal bread for feeding the holy animals so they could better digest it, but his grave expression and my earlier experience of offering unsolicited suggestions dissuaded me.

Looking for the nearby Tal Katora Lake visible on Google maps, I found that access to it was seemingly blocked by a row of houses. A group of boys and girls were inspecting one of the houses that was partially demolished for reconstruction. I asked them for directions to the lake. They suggested I pass through their house to take a view from their backyard. The offer was happily accepted.

Shivam had introduced me to Salik Khan of Jaipur, the biggest devotee of the poets Ghalib and Gulzar, as well as a learned cultural guide of his city. I met him at a busy marketplace, where I saw a cloth shop with the following words of wisdom displayed near the entrance: "Always speak sweet, so that if you have to eat your words back then they don't taste bitter."

Salik took me on a food tour. On the first day, we had dinner in what seemed like a predominantly Muslim neighbourhood of the city, called Ramganj. We feasted on a delicious curry called changezi chicken. The atmosphere in the neighbourhood on a Ramzaan night was no less electric than Old Delhi. The roads were all choking with traffic, everyone seemed to have come out to shop, eat, frolic or just watch people. Jaipur looked cleaner, neater and more organised than the cities of Uttar Pradesh.

The next day, Salik and a friend of his took me to a traditional Rajasthani-themed resort called Chokhi Dhani. It was a vast open-air space featuring art and crafts, performances and a model village. The food was uniquely Rajasthani, with the waiters insisting we had more food than our stomachs could possibly accommodate by filling our plates again and again. The glass of lassi continued getting refilled to wash down the food. Salik was upset that I did not tell him about my birthday the previous day, as he could have organised a grander celebration, whereas I thought the dinner at Chokhi Dhani was no less than a lavish feast.

Jaipur may have many attractive palaces, museums, forts and temples, but what I found most charming about the city was the manner in which the streets and squares had been named. I didn't know the story of how these names had originated but was glad that they had been retained. Some examples were Daadi ka Phatak (Grandma's Gateway), Baara Bhaiyon ka Chauraha (Crossing of the Twelve Brothers), Ghee Walon ka Raasta (Way of the ghee sellers), Khazaane Walon ka Raasta (Way of the Treasurers), Patwariyon ka Raasta (Way of the land record clerks) and the best of all,

Paagalkhaane ka Raasta (Way to the Lunatic Asylum). Then there was one that took the cake: Chatori Raandon ka Chauraha (Square of the spicy food-loving women).

While on Indian television, one is used to seeing Hindi text written in Roman letters, in the markets of Jaipur, one sees it the other way around. A lot of shop signs have English text written in Devanagari script. It was like the revenge of Devanagari script on the practice of Roman Hindi (or Romanagari, as some have started to call it).

हमारे यहाँ चोट - मोच, नाफ़,
नले, टूटी हुई हडियों का ईलाज
तसल्ली बख़्श होता है।
ख़लीफ़ा - मो. अहमद - मो. हमीद
ہمارے یہاں چوٹ ،موچ ،ناف ،نلے
ٹوٹی ہوئی ہڈیوں کا علاج تسلّی بخش ہوتا ہے
خلیفہ :: محمد احمد - محمد حمید
MOB.:- 9210782143.
"शकील" आर्ट

13

What Do They Think of Their Neighbours?

THERE IS NO BETTER WAY OF GETTING AN IDEA OF THE PERCEPTIONS OF a people than by communicating with them. So that's what I set upon doing. It did not take long to realise that in today's India, Pakistan is viewed very suspiciously. These suspicions are fuelled by the terror acts that continue to happen in India every few years. After such incidents, fingers are often pointed towards elements from Pakistan as the main culprits. This sentiment is exploited by the media and politicians in India by associating all the people from Pakistan with the actions of a few.

The reception at the hotels I stayed at in the four cities ranged from routine politeness to rather bizarre frostiness. The taxi drivers and shop attendants mostly greeted the revelation of my Pakistani identity with indifference or awkwardness.

Occasional enthusiasm was shown by some; however, they mostly turned out to be Muslims. It became obvious that Indian Muslims feeling a bond with Pakistanis is not a myth. Perhaps understandably, for what was the raison d'etre of Pakistan's creation (whether one agrees with it or not), other than to be a separate homeland for "Indian" Muslims?

One shopkeeper in Benaras said rather optimistically, in his refined accent, that ordinary Indians and Pakistanis loved each other and the tension between the two countries was simply created by the politicians. He did not acknowledge the fact that the politics of hate perpetuated by the establishment on both sides has now found a frighteningly large number of takers among the general populace.

When a taxi driver in Delhi learned that I was from Pakistan, he asked me if I was aware that some of "my people" were also in the city. Perplexed as to what he meant by "my people", I asked him what he was talking about. He told me that he had heard on TV that police had received intelligence about the arrival of some Lashkar-e-Tayyaba operatives. I spent the remainder of my journey hoping he would not turn me in at the nearest police station as one of the potential terrorists they were looking for.

Perhaps the risk of associating with a Pakistani was what prevented some of my old friends in India from inviting me to their homes for a cup of tea. What if someone from the intelligence agencies turned up to inquire what a Pakistani was doing at their house? It was very sad to realise how far and wide the fears and misgivings had spread.

The receptionist at the hotel in Agra where I stayed greeted me with a frown when I handed him my passport for check in.

"I do not understand what is it that *your country* wants," he said in Hindi. *"Bas terrorism karte rehte hain, koi development shevelopment par dhiyaan nahin hai."* (The only thing Pakistan is interested in is terrorism with no focus on development.).

The rather cold welcome form the hotel receptionist in Jaipur prompted the Muslim bellhop, who was silently observing my arrival, to remark that Muslims were being treated unfairly. Before he made this remark, he confirmed whether I was in fact from Pakistan while walking me to my room, and after making sure that we were out of his manager's earshot.

Back in Delhi, in total contrast to the abovementioned experiences, one day I received a knock at my hotel room door. I opened it to find the hotel manager on duty. He extended his hand to shake mine, saying, "Sir, I learned that there was a Pakistani guest staying at our hotel, so I thought I should shake your hand and welcome you."

The boatman in Benaras, giving me a tour in the river Ganges, had an embarrassed smile on his face as he averted his eyes when I told him I was from Pakistan. After a long pause, he recounted stories of the Pakistanis he had met when he used to work in Dubai. The moral of all his stories was that ordinary Pakistanis were just regular people, who should not be feared.

When I mentioned I was from Pakistan to a Muslim taxi driver in Jaipur, he expressed his joy at Pakistan's win over India in the ICC Champions Trophy final. "I am a big fan of Pakistan," he said.

He told me that he had wanted to set off fireworks after the win, but his father forbade him as it would have endangered peace in their neighbourhood.

At a shop in Bapu Bazaar, a Muslim shopkeeper asked me rhetorically, with a glint in his eye, about the result of the same cricket match. I said, "Of course, we won." *"Ham bhi tou jeet gaye."* (Your win is our win), he replied merrily. I found it incredible that I was experiencing this bonhomie. I wondered whether I should be happy to be experiencing it or sad that the Indian democracy had failed to integrate its Muslim population as equal stakeholders in the mainstream. What else could explain the fact that these people were not feeling a sense of belonging to the place where their lives and future belonged? Rather, what I observed was an overwhelming sense of alienation.

For my flight from Delhi to Benaras, I had to wait in a very slow-moving check-in queue at the Indira Gandhi International Airport. The man ahead of me, obviously bored and looking for someone to complain to, said, "Their systems are always down, and they are utterly incapable of making this process even slightly more efficient."

I empathised with his frustration despite having no prior experience of check ins at that airport. We engaged in a chat for as long as we were in the queue. Later in the lounge, he found me having breakfast and came to sit next to me. We continued our chat and he introduced himself as Jaswinder Singh Kooner, a musician from Punjab, who grew up in Bombay and currently lived in Delhi. During the conversation, when he noticed my Pakistani passport lying on the table along with my boarding pass, he was flummoxed.

"Oh man, you're from Pakistan, and you did not even tell me!" Jaswinder exclaimed as he shook my hand again. "So pleased to meet you, man!"

But then his expression turned a bit sombre as he lifted my passport from the table and put it in my hand, asking me to hide it in my pocket. "It is not safe to display your Pakistani identity like that. Times are bad. Not everyone will be so friendly towards you when they learn you are from Pakistan," he said.

While I was thinking about the fact that at a place as secure as an airport, an Indian was feeling insecure on my account, Jaswinder asked for my Facebook ID. He still sends me messages of greetings from time to time.

Speaking of Facebook, when I posted a few status updates about my activities in India with the hashtag #PakistaniinIndia, my Indian friends got really worried on account of my safety and I received a few messages of reprimand. They told me to spare such status updates and hashtags until my safe return to home.

In Old Delhi, I noticed a sign outside a shop, saying "Pakistani Visa Forms Available". I approached the shop attendant to ask if I could get a form. My intention was to inquire what the demand for Pakistani visa forms was like in the current environment. The man behind the counter, who had noticed me taking photos, refused to speak. He was determined to keep mum, not a word leaving his lips. His face grew tense. Perhaps he suspected some kind of mischief behind my inquiry. Maybe he thought I was a media person, trying to implicate him for association with the enemy country.

At a couple of clothing stores, I noticed signs announcing availability of Pakistani designer dresses and lawn suits. A bookshop in Delhi's Urdu Bazaar had two Urdu biographies of Quaid-e-Azam Muhammad Ali Jinnah on display. The shop next door advertised "English novels, Rs. 100 per kg". Hindi novels were substantially more expensive at Rs. 150 per kg. Another shop sign declared, "Fixed Price. No Chik-chik." At Chandni Chowk, I noticed with interest the green trilingual signboard of Indian Union Muslim League, the remnant of the party that spearheaded the campaign for the division of India.

The success of Pakistani music in capturing the imagination of Indian urbanites was evident in every city I visited. Tracks from Coke Studio, a television franchise of musical performances conceptualized in Pakistan and later replicated in India and Middle East, seemed especially popular. It was not uncommon to hear songs from the Pakistani version of Coke Studio being played at cafés and restaurants in Delhi and Jaipur. At a restaurant in Mehrauli, I overheard a conversation by a group sitting at a table near us, about how the music churned out by Pakistani Coke Studio was far superior to that of its Indian counterpart.

शुभ
लाभ
SK.
Art 9305045534

ماہر امراض پوشدہ وماہر ختنہ
Fena
Fena
Fena
फेना ही लेना

14

The Lives and Times of the Muslims of India

SOME OF MY INDIAN FRIENDS REMAINED NERVOUS ABOUT MY CARE-free wanderings and cautioned me not to flaunt my Pakistani identity, considering the environment of heightened animosity between the two countries. Another newly made friend had warned me that as a Muslim Pakistani, I remained the perfect candidate for getting lynched. For me, however, the whole experience of visiting India would have lost half its meaning if I were to desist from declaring where I had come from.

Among the numerous *ghats* by the bank of Ganges in Benaras, a mosque stands out due to its domes and minarets. Known as Alamgir Mosque, it was built during the reign of Mughal emperor Aurangzeb over the ruins of a Hindu temple. While today its presence amongst the *ghats* makes the resplendent architectural landscape of the riverbank even more striking, one can understand that, for some Hindus, it stands as an unpleasant reminder of the destruction of their places of worship by Muslim rulers.

Being the lone visitor on a hot summer afternoon, a member of the mosque's administration invited me to his office-cum-living quarters. He had seen how uncomfortably I was walking barefoot on the hot floor of the courtyard. I accepted his invitation instantly. The room had a cool cement floor and was decorated with some very basic furniture. The man, who introduced himself as the muezzin of the mosque, turned on the small electric room cooler. I sat on the old cane chair by the door as he reclined on a cot in front of me, propping himself up with his elbow on a cushion. The ticking of the wall clock was audible. Next to it hung a calendar with images of the green-domed Prophet's Mosque in Medina and some calligraphed Quranic verses. The place felt tranquil.

I asked him about how it felt to have their place of worship surrounded by the holiest sites of Hindu faith.

"Arre sahab, dab ke nahin rehte ham" (We don't live under any fear), he proclaimed without hesitation. "The proportion of Muslim population in the city is equal to that of the Hindus now," he added.

I found that claim a tad outlandish. He praised the Muslim community of the city for its high literacy rate and even higher birth rate, with the amusing addition, *"Hamare musalmaan larkon ki personality bhi zyada achhi hai.*" (Our Muslim boys have more well-groomed personalities.)

He went on to make another statement, while eyeing me with a probing look, "*Ham ne suna hai batwaare ke waqt Pakistan ke hisse mein bohat thore musalmaan aaye the, zyada toh yaheen India mein rahe,*" (I have heard that Pakistan received a very small share of the Muslim population of United India at the time of Partition; the majority of them remained in India).

I offered my own perspective. "Pakistanis have proven to be more fertile, since independence, than their brethren this side of the border, as evidenced by our steep population growth rate. If there was any shortfall in our numbers, it has been more than made up by now."

Not looking very convinced, he changed the subject by offering to let me take a panoramic view of the city from the roof of the mosque for a fee of 200 rupees.

***

"*Dab ke nahin rehte ham*" was a statement I had heard from Muslims on a number of occasions in the four cities of India that I visited. In the context of the current times, I wondered if it was their mantra for self-assurance and shaking off of fear.

Interestingly, Muslims are often referred to as Mohammedans (pronounced *Momdans*) in India. The term coined by the British is still prevalent and is used by Muslims and non-Muslims alike, while it has gone completely out of vogue in Pakistan and the rest of the world.

Did the difference in reaction of Indian Muslims to my Pakistani identity, compared to those who did not share my religious identity, indicate their sincere love for Pakistan or was it just a reaction to the rising trend of right-wing Hindu nationalism and their resultant sense of alienation? An Indian friend said things had not been so bad before BJP came into power in 2014. During their rule, majoritarian ideology pervaded the media and public discourse, which had a deeply polarising effect on the society. "Extreme sentiments have taken hold among people lately. They look at people of other communities suspiciously, pointing to the success of the Hindu hyper-nationalist project underway under the aegis the current Indian government."

I asked Salik Khan for his perspective, who had earlier declared me ripe for lynching. He agreed with the sense of disaffection among Muslims but added that Muslims were still undoubtedly better off living in India than in Pakistan. "Indian constitution enshrines guarantees for all citizens regardless of their faith. The same cannot be said of Pakistani laws which institutionalise preferential treatment for the majority faith," he said. "True, we have had our Gujarat pogrom but do not forget that thousands upon thousands of fellow Bengali Muslims were killed and raped at the hands of the Pakistani military."

The perspective that surprised me was of another gentleman I met in Delhi. He said Pakistan was to blame for the rise of Hindu hard right in India. "The series of high-profile terrorist attacks carried out on Indian soil by Pakistan-backed militants was one of the major reasons for Hindu hard right's consolidation of power. The BJP based its political rhetoric on the question of national security, for which adopting an aggressive and antagonistic stance towards Pakistan was vital. Anyone speaking of peace building measures is termed as enemy of the state."

Enter Rishi Raj Singh, a decade-old acquaintance from the virtual world of social media. Before Facebook, there was a social networking website by the name of orkut. India Pakistan Friendship Club (IPFC) was an open public community on orkut dedicated to promoting peace between the two countries. In reality, you were more likely to find members bickering with each other in defence of their national narratives. Fed up with the incessant bickering by commoners from both countries, "IPFC Snobs" emerged as a breakaway community, membership to which was by invitation only. Here, Indians and Pakistanis who prided themselves on being more learned and perceptive, engaged in civilised debates. This was where I was first introduced to Rishi.

Engaging in discussions on internet forums in those days helped one understand that our places of origin should not necessarily be the determinants of our worldviews. The views we have learned from textbooks and inherited from our communities are not necessarily always the right ones. By speaking with and listening to "others", appreciating their opinions and empathising with them becomes possible.

Rishi had told me then about one of his schoolteachers whose surname, Khandapur, sounded similar to mine. Despite the phonetic similarity, there was no connection between us, however. Still, in those days when my access to good historical resources was limited, coupled with immense curiosity about the history of my clan, I asked him to find that teacher and connect me with her.

While that connection was never established, I surely did meet up with Rishi in Delhi, who travelled some distance to come and see me. From his recent social media posts, I had noticed a change in his views, which were had become very right-wing and therefore unsympathetic towards Pakistan and Pakistanis.

"I have become very extreme in my views," Rishi admitted. "But I feel guilty when I meet people like you as well as my old Muslim friends, who are still very kind to me, despite being aware of my Hindu supremacist views."

I was intrigued by his disarming confession. How complex are the ways of one's conscience that it can make one feel guilty of one's views and still push one to stand by the same views? In any case his admission served to break the ice. We spoke about old times and departed on pleasant terms.

Another old acquaintance from the days of orkut, who came to meet me at the hotel in Delhi and gifted me his newly published book, surprised me the most with his social media posts over the coming months and years. During our meeting, he had said that he was facing the wrath of *bhakts* (a term that has come to be associated with diehard supporters of BJP and other Hindu nationalist parties), because he had promised to donate profits from his book sales to the cause of promoting girls' education in the "backward" Muslim communities. Years later, I observed a sea change in his attitude, as he regularly resorted to vilifying Muslims in his social media posts. At the anniversary of Babri Masjid's demolition, he made a post to celebrate it and vowed that all such reminders of the rule of "foreigners" over India would be eliminated one by one.

Bizarrely, it was during my visit of India that I witnessed the surreal spectacle of a group, going by the name of Hindu Sena, throwing a birthday bash in honour of the then US President Donald Trump at Jantar Mantar in Delhi. Announcements for the birthday bash described the US President as "the saviour of humanity". What could explain the excitement and support for Trump among the right-wing Hindu groups? His rhetoric of banning Muslims from entering the United States surely had something to do with it.

Muslims in Jaipur celebrating Pakistan's victory in a cricket match and Hindus in Delhi celebrating Donald Trump's birthday – the similarity was obvious in the concept of your enemy's enemy being your friend. There were many enlightening and thought-provoking phenomena at work in India for those who cared to pause, observe and perceive.

THE PRICE OF LOOKING
OF SILENCE

15

The Grave of My Idol

I REGRETTED THAT I COULD NOT MEET HER WHILE SHE WAS ALIVE. Now that I was in her country, I wanted to at least pay my respects at places associated with her memory.

I am talking about the matchless Urdu novelist and short-story writer, Qurratulain Hyder. She remains my all-time favourite writer in any language.

I headed towards the graveyard of Jamia Millia Islamia. I had read in newspaper reports at the time of her death in 2007 that this was her final resting place. From the auto I was travelling in, I noticed a gate with her name displayed in bold letters above it. I told the driver that I wanted to get off right there. I thought since the university had honoured the late author by naming one of its entrances after her, it must also house some useful resources and memorabilia relating to her.

I passed through the gate and entered a small office nearby, which appeared to deal with security and administration matters. I asked the man sitting across the table if he knew of any Qurratulain Hyder-related material housed anywhere on the campus.

"Who, Qurratulain Hyder?" he asked with the sort of annoyance reserved for visitors with stupid inquiries.

"The one after whom this gate is named," I replied.

"I don't know, mister. I just know about this gate." The matter was concluded.

I proceeded towards the cemetery alone, but once I reached, its immense size confounded me. How was I going to find her grave in a sprawling cemetery that seemed to contain a million and one graves? I asked a man who looked like a caretaker if he knew its location. He was utterly clueless. With no pointers, the task ahead looked daunting.

While contemplating my mission, I walked on, reading inscriptions on tombstones. I saw one that had "Amma" (Mother) engraved on it. Without revealing the name of the grave's occupant, the inscription was laden with emotional tributes from the children of the deceased.

The goddess of luck must have decided to favour me in that moment, because the very next tombstone that caught my eye happened to be the one I had come to look for. Had I been unlucky, I could have searched all day before finding it, or worse, I could have started my search from the other end of the cemetery and not found it at all. The tombstone read: "Qurratulain Hyder, daughter of Syed Sajjad Hyder Yildrim. Date of birth: 20th January 1927. Date of death: 21st August 2007"

The grave of the greatest Urdu novelist had a simple unassuming plaque at one end and nothing to cover its barren soil. I sat there in silence, amidst the sea of the dead, reflecting on the journey of those that floated on the ocean of time before us and sailed into the sunset. What was my connection with the one who lay in the unadorned grave by which I sat? The dead one lived on in the memories I was carrying – memories of the world weaved through her stories, her characters that had cast their spell on me. From the haze of those memories materialized these few lines on her favourite subject of time, as if addressed to me:

"Why is this man sitting here? Why do we all find ourselves at this specific place in this particular moment? How did the different pieces of life's puzzle come together to create this pattern? Something is going to happen. Some event, that will cause the pieces of this puzzle to be scattered. But the flight of time will create yet another puzzle. Someone will try to solve it too. But we won't be here to witness it. Time will move on. The desire to live, the desire to be happy, the magnetic wave of life will be lost in the wilderness of time. These helpless little people – what do the coming times have in store for them? What will their eyes see? How will their hearts beat? Nobody knows why all of this is the way it is." – *Mere Bhi Sanamkhaane* (My Idol Houses Too).

I wondered if the university had a section dedicated to her work. I asked a watchman if there was an Urdu department. He directed me towards the block that housed it. Upon entering the building, I saw a few men working at their desks. I announced the purpose of my visit hesitantly, addressing no one in particular. One of them directed me to go upstairs.

Upstairs, I found three gentlemen and one lady. As I repeated the announcement I had made downstairs, they eyed me with curiosity. I was looking for resources about Qurratulain Hyder. They asked me whether I was a journalist or a researcher. I told them I was a chartered accountant, hailing from Dera Ismail Khan, living in London, who was just passionate about the works of Qurratulain Hyder.

Another gentleman, who was quietly listening to the conversation until that point, revealed that he had written two books on her works. He introduced himself as Dr. Anwar ul Haque. My mission was seeing its first sign of success. The lady in the room suggested that I should meet the chairman of the department and asked a staff member to accompany me to his office downstairs. Dr. Anwar ul Haque had to leave, so I took his number, hoping to arrange a meeting with him later.

Back downstairs, I entered the chairman's office, where he sat behind a large desk covered with a glass, signing away documents while an assistant by his side turned each page, pointing to the spot on the paper where the signatures should be scribbled. Some Urdu professors or lecturers were also sitting on the sofas nearby. I had to awkwardly announce my introduction to get their attention, and their attention I did get when I told them where I had come from.

Questions about my background and the intent of my visit were repeated. I was pleasantly surprised that all of them had heard of my hometown Dera Ismail Khan, as if people from there visited their office every day. Noticing my interest, the professors started recounting stories and memories of well-known Urdu authors.

The chairman Mr. Shehpar Rasool related that the renowned progressive Pakistani poet, Fahmida Riaz, used to work at Jamia during her exile in India. Another professor commented that her bold political commentary often used to make the university administration uneasy. I had a close connection with Fahmida Riaz, who was alive at the time, so I listened to the gossip with interest, thinking I would report it to her when I called on her next.

Another professor remarked that Pakistan's female poets were far too outspoken and liberal in their thoughts and lifestyles.

"Itni azaad khayal toh yahaan ki Hindi auratein bhi nahin hoteen, kuja ke Musalman khawateen" (Even Hindi (sic) women here are not so liberal in their thoughts, let alone the Muslim women). There was mention of Kishwar Naheed, Parveen Shakir, Zehra Nigah and a few others.

Fascinating observations, I thought. I reminded them about the purpose of my visit. One of them recalled the existence of Qurratulain Hyder's archives at the university but was not sure of its location. They decided to send me to a library in another block on the campus, with a staff member escorting me.

We found the very polite and welcoming librarian reading a book of Quranic verses, titled *"Pakistani Panjsurah"* in his office. Since it was the month of Ramzaan, it was not an uncommon sight to find people reading Quran in shops, markets, and now in the library. The librarian took me to a room and unlocked the door for me.

I could not believe my eyes! The room housed Qurratulain Hyder's bookcases, paintings, furniture, awards and albums. It was an overwhelming experience. I felt like I was inside her Noida home that I had only seen in documentaries and interviews. Every object looked familiar to me. On the walls hung some paintings and sketches she had made with her hands. There were photographs of her parents and uncles and of her beloved home in Lucknow that features in her stories. Awards and trophies conferred by presidents and prime ministers were arranged on top of a sideboard. A small bookshelf held her collection of books and journals. Another cabinet contained her tea set and porcelain statues. There was a cane armchair that she used to sit on. It felt like her words were reverberating in that little room in her own voice. I wanted to spend hours listening to, reading and examining all the items, but time is never enough on such occasions. When the time came, I left with a feeling of exhilaration that my visit turned out to be more fruitful than I could have ever dreamed.

इश्क मुझको नहीं, वहशत
मेरी वहशत तेरी शोहरत
be madly in love with you,
not call it madness, and frown.
And should it be madness, don't forget:
It brought you your renown!
कहूँ किससे मै के क्या है, शब-ए-ग़म दुरी बला है
मुझे क्या बुरा था मरना, अगर एक बार होता?
This night of my suffering, away from you,
is dying many deaths in a row.
I'll gladly welcome Death, for it
would strike once, then no more.
ये कहाँ कि दोस्ती है, के बने है दोस्त नासेह?
कोई चारासाज़ होता, कोई ग़मगुसार होता
O preacher, all your words well-meant
give me no comfort of a friend.
For me, my friends are only those
who tend and heal my woes.
ATLAS

16

Following the Trail of Urdu

THE FIRST NOTICEABLE THING FOR ME WHEN I ARRIVED IN DELHI WAS the multilingual road signs. They are written in English, Hindi, Urdu and Punjabi (Gurmukhi script), the four official languages of the National Capital Territory. Seeing Urdu on the road signs was reassuring, for Pakistanis often like to unnecessarily worry themselves with the plight of Urdu in its birthplace and attribute to it an exclusive Pakistani identity, even though it is not native to any of the provinces that eventually made up Pakistan.

Urdu signboards and posters were also very common in Old Delhi in the form of shop signs or advertising banners; however, in the other three cities I visited, Benaras, Agra and Jaipur, Urdu in public places was a rare sight. In the state of Uttar Pradesh, where Benaras and Agra are located, it enjoys the status of being the second official language after Hindi.

How could the visit to Delhi be worthwhile without a pilgrimage to Ghalib's haveli? It was fascinating to see how the haveli in Gali Qasim Jan had been turned into a museum of sorts, with free entry. My friend, Arunav, and I were the only visitors there at the time. The displays included some utensils, garments and other household items that had not in fact belonged to Ghalib but were supposed to simulate what Ghalib would have used. Accounts of Ghalib's life and some of his well-known poetic verses were written on signboards along with some pictures and sketches of him. On one wall hung a framed print of first day cover issued by Pakistan Post Office on the occasion of Ghalib's death centenary in 1969. The word 'Pakistan' was written on the stamps in Urdu, Bengali and English.

Inside the haveli, there was a travel agent's office on one side, which looked very out of place. Reading the trilingual plaque which had a short bio of Ghalib written on it, Arunav exclaimed in disbelief, "Ghalib was married to Umrao Jaan!" thinking of the famous character from Mirza Ruswa's novel of the same name, and perhaps visualising the actress Rekha as Ghalib's wife, who had played Umrao Jaan's role in the film adaptation.

When I read it closely, I realised the Urdu text had Ghalib's wife's name written correctly as "Umrao Begum" but the person writing the English text perhaps got carried away with the same visualisation as my friend.

From another plaque, I read aloud Ghalib's couplet:

Koi veerani si veerani hai
Ghar ko dekh kar dasht yaad aaya
(Is there any wilderness more desolate than this?
The sight of home reminds me of the desert)

I noticed that words had been switched around incorrectly in the second line of Urdu text, but the Hindi text had it written correctly as "*Dasht ko dekh ke ghar yaad aaya.*" (The sight of the desert reminds me of home).

These glaring errors in Ghalib's bio and poetry right inside his haveli should have been outrageous, but I could not help finding them comical.

Ghalib's tomb is located at quite a distance from his haveli, near the dargah of Hazrat Nizamuddin Auliya. A white marble mausoleum was built on his grave almost a century after his death. Located adjacent to the mausoleum is Ghalib Academy. The three-storey building of the academy houses a library, an auditorium and a museum in honour of the life and times of the most famous poet in the Urdu language.

The most amusing item on display in the museum is a sitting life-size statue of Ghalib in his old age, smoking a hookah, while a courtesan in a dancing pose stands behind him wearing heavy jewellery. Perhaps she was Nawaab Jaan, a dancing girl madly in love with Ghalib's poetry and by extension, his person.

In the library of Ghalib's Academy, I was surprised to see many Urdu daily newspapers scattered on the reading tables. It presented a completely different picture to the common lament about the decline of Urdu. Were those papers doing good business? The fact that they were in circulation meant that they had enough subscribers to make them commercially viable. Perhaps, there were still sanctuaries like Ghalib Academy where Urdu was safe from the effects of decline, at least so far. The surrounding shelves were filled with Urdu books on a variety of topics, but predominantly religion, poetry and society.

Later in Old Delhi, while walking along the Urdu Bazaar Road outside the Jama Masjid, I spotted an Urdu signboard reading "Daagh Academy" with a picture of the famous Urdu poet Daagh. My curiosity was aroused, and I wanted to find out what the Academy named after another of my favourite Urdu poets was all about. The people manning the bookstores stocking Urdu books beneath the signboard disappointed me by saying they had no clue about it.

"Go up the stairs and find out for yourself," advised one. Atop the narrow staircase, I found myself between two doors. Not knowing which one was the right one, I knocked on the one to my right. A lady's voice from behind the door asked, "*Kaun hai?*" (Who is there?).

Awkwardly, I laid bare the purpose of my visit.

"Knock on the door to your left," said the same voice from behind the door.

When I did as I was instructed, a man emerged and invited me in. It was an empty house which was being repainted. The man who had let me in was supervising the workers. His name was

Muhammad Qasim Dehlavi. He informed me that he ran the academy and had launched a magazine on Daagh that published articles on poetic and literary topics in Urdu. I bought a copy of it.

It was this same magazine that I carried into Khawaja Bakhtiyar Kaki's dargah later that evening, when a woman mistook it for a *siparah* (a Quranic chapter) and chastised me softly for holding it in the same hand as my shoes that I had taken off to enter the dargah.

A few days later, I met Dr. Anwarul Haque of Jamia Millia Islamia near his home in the very crowded neighbourhood of Jamia Nagar. He gifted me a copy of his book on Qurratulain Hyder's non-fiction prose work. He would not hear of receiving payment for it.

Frenzied shopping was taking place all around in Jamia Nagar. A banner for kurta pajama and "Pathani suit" hung over the street. On one wall a poster reading "*Rishte hi Rishte*" (Lots of marriage proposals) advertised matrimonial services. On another wall, a poster advertised industrial-sized weighing scales, "*Kaante hi kaante*" (Lots of heavy-duty weighing scales).

A little further on, black graffiti on a red brick wall was visible between many posters. The Hindi text read: "*Yahaan peshaab karna sakht manaa hai. Jurmaana 200 rupay. Gadhe ke poot, yahaan mat moot*" (Urinating here is strictly forbidden. Fine Rs. 200. Son of an ass, don't pee here.) Visual and olfactory evidence suggested that the warnings had failed miserably in deterring offenders.

Not far from there, I met Shiraz Husain, the creator of Khwaab Tanha Collective. Though I had seen images of Shiraz's wonderful art, it was Salik who introduced me to him. When I texted Shiraz asking to meet him, he wanted to know why. Once satisfied that it was only to see and talk about his work, he invited me to his home.

Shiraz had embarked upon a one-of-a-kind venture, making Urdu poetry and prose themed artwork. His paintings usually depict sketches of the poet or author along with snippets of their poetry or quotes. The excerpts are also written in Devanagari and Roman alphabet along with the original Urdu text, to broaden their understanding and appeal. These paintings are converted into posters, postcards, T-shirts, satchels and mugs. It is heartening to note that several such ventures have since been launched in India to make Urdu literature available to a wider audience with the help of multimedia.

Shiraz's mother also entered the living room and addressed me in a very loving manner. "*Kahan se aaya hai yeh bacha*?" (Where has this kid come from?) she asked Shiraz. She sat down next to me and recollected how her family had been split at the time of Partition, leaving behind an enduring legacy of pain. Shiraz let me collect as many posters as I wanted to take home. He also would not hear of receiving payment, despite my insistence.

D. I. KHAN B. S.
SECONDARY
R - BLOCK,
NEW DELHI - 110060
Bohrianwala Thalia Complex, Inder Puri
GOSWAMI SATI KEWALRAMJI (BOHRIANWALA) MEMORIAL SOCIETY
D.I.KHAN BHARATRI
SR. SEC. SCHOOL

17

Traces of My Hometown in a Foreign Land

WHEN I FIRST GOT ACQUAINTED WITH THE INTERNET, I STARTED probing it for any resources it contained about my hometown. During one such search many moons ago when I used to live in Islamabad, I came across an unexpected find: a school in Delhi called D. I. Khan Senior Secondary School.

For the first time, I was alerted to the possibility of a community in India that could have migrated from my hometown

– their hometown – at the time of Partition and kept their identity alive by christening institutions in its name.

A few years later, in the earliest days of social media, when an online platform called orkut emerged on the scene, I used it to make friends across the border. I sought their help to determine if that school was actually named after Dera Ismail Khan or if it was a mere coincidence that the acronym was similar. The disadvantage of having a long name is to have it frequently subjected to acronymization. The case of my hometown was even more unfortunate since it could be reduced to DIK. My virtual friends did not prove to be of much help, though; perhaps for good reason, as I was meant to visit the institution and find out for myself one day.

Before I proceed with this account, a bit of background information is in order. My hometown Dera Ismail Khan is the principal city in the southernmost district of Khyber Pakhtunkhwa province in Pakistan. It has remained the closest settled district next to the erstwhile tribal agencies of Waziristan. For centuries, it served as a key stop this side of the Suleiman Mountain range for Afghan *powindah* (nomadic) traders. It remained a key trading city even after a border was formally established between British India and Afghanistan, and until a couple of decades after the creation of Pakistan. Before Partition, a third of the city's population were Hindus. The oldest natives of the city speak Seraiki (which used to be more commonly known as Derawali or Hindko locally) and around a third of the population have Pashto as their first language. Tehsil Kulachi, my ancestral village, falls within the Dera Ismail Khan district and also used to have a sizable Hindu population before Partition.

A few years ago, I came across a documentary titled *Dere tun Dilli* (Dera to Delhi). It was a moving account of the chronicles and memories of the generation that had to leave their homes and possessions in Dera Ismail Khan to settle in Delhi as refugees in the aftermath of Partition. It showed how the older generation had tried their best to preserve their Derawali language (the name by which Seraiki was known in the region before the broader Seraiki appellation became commonplace), folk songs and cultural ethos and thus creating a little piece of Dera in Delhi. However, as the older generations passed on and younger ones took their place, the sense of association with Derawal identity, traditions and customs was slowly being lost.

I had seen Shilpi Gulati's name in the credits of the documentary. Before arriving in Delhi, I managed to get in touch with her and we met at a café in Khan Market. I asked her how the idea of the documentary was conceptualised. She told me how she grew up in a world where the specific ethnic identity of Derawali speakers became overshadowed by Punjabi. Later in life, when she became conscious of Derawali's distinctiveness, she embarked upon this project to document snippets of the older generation's memories of their beloved city, its bazaars, food, language and songs.

It warms my heart every time I watch the documentary, to see people reminisce about life as it used to be in Dera Ismail Khan until 1947, before the exile forced upon its Hindu inhabitants. They did not know at the time that the break with their homeland would be permanent. Derawals that settled in Delhi stuck together as a community, formed associations, organised events, established schools and temples, brought out magazines and never forgot the home they left behind. In the words of one elderly gentleman featured in the documentary, "You have taken away my country, my home. But you cannot take away my memories. At least those are my own."

Shilpi told me a sweet account of an uncle who made it his mission to compile the contact details of everyone hailing from Dera Ismail Khan by going from house to house. He wanted to make a directory of Derawals settled all over India. It was like a fight to preserve something precious from its impending erasure. The forces of time, however, eventually do their work by enforcing separations and loosening bonds that would have once been considered permanent. As the narrator says:

"In the memory of my grandparents, Delhi mirrors Dera. Dera has lived on in their hearts, in their words, in their songs. They have spent their lives calling both places home. Memory is made by us as much as it makes us. So much or so little is filtered through a single story. Yet single stories add up to a collective memory. And it is unnerving to realise that within the next decade or so, these stories, the collective memory of an entire community, will be completely lost."

Shilpi told me that many of the elders of the community interviewed in the documentary had already passed away, including her grandfather, to whose memory it was dedicated. On her part, after having made this invaluable contribution to preserve the community's heritage, Shilpi did not want to keep dwelling in the past and was ready to move on.

GOSWAMI SATI KEWALRAMJI
BOHRIANWALA THALLA
INDERPURI N DELHI

۱۷ر دسمبر ۸۲ء 13 V. Imp

بسم اللہ الرحمٰن الرحیم

عنایت اللہ خاں
گنڈہ پور کالج - گنڈہ پور - کلاچی
ڈیرہ اسماعیل خاں - فون نمبر ۲

۱۵ نومبر ۱۹۸۲ء

نہایت پیارے بھائی لالہ نخت رام جی سلامت رہو

میری دعا ہے کہ آپ ہمیشہ بخیریت، تندرست اور خوش حال رہیں۔

آپ اندازہ نہیں کر سکتے کہ بھائی دیوی دیال صاحب کے آنے - ملنے سے ہمیں کتنی خوشی ہوئی - ہمیں یقین ہے کہ جتنا پ سے ملنے کا شوق ہے اُتنا آپ کو بھی ہو گا - لیکن مشکلات راہ میں حائل ہیں لیکن اللہ کی رحمت سے مایوسی و نہیں سکتی - آپ کے پتا جی اور بھائی کی وفات کا سُن کر بہت افسوس ہوا - آپ کو یہ سُنکر رنج ہو گا کہ میرے والد اور دونوں بڑے بھائی عطا اللہ خاں اور عصمت اللہ خاں بھی اللہ کو پیارے ہو گئے اور اسی راستہ ہم ن کو جانا ہے -

آپ سے ملنے کو بہت جی چاہتا ہے - ہماری دعا ہے کہ اللہ تعالیٰ آپ سب کو خوش و خرم رکھے - اگر کسی سے - کلاچی والے دوست سے ملاقات ہو تو میری طرف سے ان کو گلے لگا کر سلام کریں اور پیار کریں - ن واقعات اور حالات میں کچھ زیادہ کہنا آپ کے لئے اور ہمارے لئے مشکلات کا باعث بن سکتا ہے - ہا ہے کہ جو جذبات میرے دل میں ہیں - آپ کے لئے اور یہاں سے جانے والوں کے لئے ہیں ویسے محبت اور جذبات آپ کے دلوں میں بھی ہوں گے - اور ان حالات میں سوائے دعاؤں اور نیک خواہشات کے کچھ ہ بھی نہیں -

ہری دعا ہے کہ اللہ تعالیٰ آپ کو خوش و خرم، شاد و آباد رکھے -

ر قسمت میں ملاقات ہوئی تو دل کھول کر باتیں کریں گے -

طالب خیریت

خیر اندیش عنایت اللہ خاں گنڈہ پور

وٹ :-

مندرجہ بالا خط شری نخت رام جی کے دوست سردار عنایت اللہ خاں گنڈہ پور (کلاچی کی نواب فیملی سے) کا تحریر شدہ ہے - سردار عنایت اللہ خاں صاحب صوبہ سرحد کے وزیر اعلیٰ (چیف منسٹر) بھی رہے - انہوں نے راقم کی بھی بہت خاطر تواضع کی - راقم والی بال کلب کا سکریٹری تھا اور وہ صدر ہوا کرتے تھے -

راقم دیوی دیال کھانیجو

18

Continuing the Dera Ismail Khan Investigation

I WENT TO VISIT THE SCHOOL WITH THE NAME THAT HAD FIRST alerted me to the existence of a Derawal community in Delhi: D. I. Khan Bharatri Sabha Senior Secondary School in Rajinder Nagar. I was received very warmly by the manager of the school, Mr. Vijay Kumar Taneja, whom I had contacted in advance. Also hailing from the Kulachi tehsil of Dera Ismail Khan district, Mr. Taneja knew the Pashtun tribe of Gandapurs very well. He gave me a tour of the school. I saw plaques bearing names of various people from the community who had contributed to the establishment and running of the school. Each plaque had "of D. I. Khan" or "of Kulachi" inscribed beneath the name of the person it commemorated.

The school was established in the mid-1950s. Its logo included the Sanskrit text "*Tamaso Ma Jyotir Gamaya*". The school's principal told me that it was a prayer from the Upanishads meaning, "Lead us from darkness to light". I told them of the Quranic verse "*Min az zulumaati il an noor*" (From darkness to light) that was part of the logo of a public school I had studied at in Kohat, Pakistan. The message in the prayers and their placement was identical.

After completing the tour of his school, Mr. Taneja drove me to the second school run by the D. I. Khan community, called Sati Kewal Ram (SKR) Public School, named after a 17th-century Hindu saint who had established his base in a village near Dera.

The school compound included a small temple. At the base of a tree outside the temple, a sign read that the sapling for it had been brought from Bilot, the village near Dera where the original temple of Sati Kewal Ram was located. Mr. Arjun Kumar Arora, the chairman of the school, related the story of the sapling's journey. It was brought to Delhi from Dera with the help of Sikh pilgrims who had gone to visit their holy sites in Pakistan.

Inside the chairman's office, a faded black and white group photo hung on the wall. The caption read 'Government High School Kulachi, 1944-45'. Was it a picture of my forefathers and their playmates? It appeared to be a graduation photo, with senior management and guests sitting on chairs in the front row, some students squatting on the ground, two of them reclining on their elbows in opposite directions to create a symmetrical formation, and several turbaned gents standing in the back row. I recognised the name and title of a great grand-uncle of mine at the bottom: Shah Alam Khan, Director of Education. He must have been invited as a guest to the graduation ceremony. I could have never imagined that I would find a picture of my kin proudly displayed on the wall of a school in Delhi, yet there I was, spellbound at having had such an experience in the unlikeliest of places! In that moment, it seemed like the seven decades between us had evaporated and I was present among my own people.

Mr. Arora was busy giving instructions to his staff. At his desk, I found an issue of a fortnightly magazine called *Sati Kewal Ram Hind Sandesh*. It seemed like a newsmagazine, covering local events, news and community reports, with content in English, Hindi and one page in Urdu.

I asked for the archives of the magazine's old issues. A box was brought and placed on the table with bound issues from the 1970s and 1980s. A gradual decline in Urdu content over the decades was noticeable as I flicked through the pages. Whereas Urdu text dominated most of the pages in the older issues, it was now relegated to a single page in the new issues, usually containing a poem. This was a reflection of the decline of Urdu's status from a language of correspondence, law and commerce to one good for exotic poetic expression only.

Casually turning the pages of an old issue, I came across a marvellous find: A letter in Urdu from a well-known late elder of the Gandapur clan, former chief minister of Khyber-Pakhtunkhwa, Inayatullah Khan Gandapur, addressed to his childhood pal, Lala Takhat Ram, one of the founders of the educational institutions established by the Derawal community in Delhi.

It was a letter written by one long lost friend to another, sent via a visitor to Kulachi from India, with the intent of rekindling contact after more than three decades. Following the established etiquette, the author of the letter started by sending his condolences over the death of the recipient's family members, the news of which had reached him and, in the same vein, informed him about the deaths in his own family. Published in the December 1982 issue of the magazine, it was a beautiful short memo, holding a lot of tenderness, goodwill and nostalgia. Inayatullah Khan Gandapur wrote (translated from Urdu):

15 November 1982

My extremely dear brother, Lala Takhat Ram Jee, may you stay in safety!

I pray to Almighty Allah to always keep you happy and healthy.

You cannot imagine how happy I was at the arrival of brother, Devi Dayal Jee. I am sure that as much as we yearn to meet you, you also long to meet us, but there are hurdles in the way. However, it is impossible to lose faith in the benevolence of Allah. I was very saddened to learn about the death of your Pita Jee (father) and brother. You will be sad to know that my father and both elder brothers also surrendered their lives to Allah. That's the path every human being must follow.

I am so keen to meet you. I pray again that God may keep all of you happy and healthy. If you meet an old friend or a brother from Kulachi, please embrace him on my behalf, pay my regards and convey my love.

In the current circumstances, saying more than that could result in difficulties for both you and us. I believe that the sentiments of love and friendship we hold for you and others who had to leave their homes here (during Partition) are reciprocated by you in equal measure. In these times, nothing else seems possible except exchanging prayers and best wishes for each other.

If fate had a reunion in store for us, we would chat freely to our hearts' content.

Sincerely yours,

Inayatullah Khan Gandapur

***

I turned the pages, moved by the emotions so vividly expressed in the letter, and found this Urdu couplet in another article:

Ay Zauq kisi hamdam-e-deireena ka milna
Behtar hai mulaqaat e maseeha o khizr se
(Reunion with a friend from old times is a treat
Better than meetings with messiahs and saints)

The two gentlemen passed away before fate could provide the occasion for a reunion.

समिति भवन
आई. खान सेवा समिति (पंजी.)
सेवा समिति मार्ग, डेरावाल नगर, दिल्ली
27111850
सेवा समिति भवन
डी.आई. खान सेवा समिति (रजि.)
रिश्ते-नाते सेवा
(निःशुल्क)
घोषणा

19

Who Lives in Derawal Nagar After All?

ANOTHER DAY AND ANOTHER CLUE TO INVESTIGATE IN MY PURSUIT OF signs of Dera Ismail Khan in Delhi. My next stop was a neighbourhood by the name of Derawal Nagar, a name that held a lot of promise. I had read a brief one-line description of this place somewhere on the internet, that it was a housing colony established by the Indian government to settle refugees from the Derajat (a historical cultural region in present-day Pakistan, comprising the divisions of Dera Ismail Khan and Dera Ghazi Khan). But why did the government feel the need to have a separate neighbourhood for the people of the Derajat? Did they create separate neighbourhoods for immigrants from every district?

On the road to Derawal Nagar, I read the following lines on the back of a truck, "*Buri nazar wale, tera munh kaala*" (May the face of the one casting an evil eye be blackened). Such witty one-liners are also commonly found on the backs of trucks and rickshaws in Pakistan. A tailor was working on his sewing machine by the roadside under the shade of an umbrella, wiping sweat off his face.

I arrived at the housing colony. Walking in the street along the rows of houses, I could not find anything that distinguished the neighbourhood from any other. I asked a couple of passers-by about the history of the neighbourhood. They were clueless.

That was not a surprise, though. Among the Derawals in Delhi, those who had actually spent time in Dera Ismail Khan before Partition and remembered it were on the verge of extinction. The owners and occupants of the houses must have changed in the last seven decades. Perhaps the new residents did not care about the origin of their neighbourhood's name.

In a side street, I came across a real estate broker's office. I walked in and informed the man inside about the important mission I was on. He proved to be helpful. He directed me to a Hindu temple two streets away where, according to him, I would have a good chance of finding the oldest inhabitants of the colony. I walked to the temple and saw a Hindi signboard on the adjacent building, saying "D. I. Khan Sewa Samiti" (D. I. Khan Service Organisation). It looked like I had found the place I was looking for.

I stepped into the building and found myself in what looked like an administrative office. Framed photographs of important people from the community adorned the walls, some of them garlanded. "Of D. I. Khan" was written below the names of most. The gentleman sitting behind the desk looked incredulous when I told him that I had come from the city after which the whole neighbourhood had been named and built.

Phone calls were made, more folks from the community were called in, tea was ordered and kachoris were served to the man from Dera Ismail Khan, who had come to meet the natives of his city who had been forcibly separated from it.

One young man went out to fetch the only elderly gentleman of the neighbourhood, who had actually "lived" in Dera Ismail Khan. When he arrived, he embraced me. He said he was only five years old when his family left home, leaving behind all their possessions in the mass exodus of Hindus from the land they had lived in for generations.

"Do you know about Sotay Wali Gali?" he asked. "That's where our house was." He went on to ask if the said street and house still existed. I assured him I would look for it on my next visit to my hometown – his hometown.

One gentleman in the gathering said, "The Muslims of Dera were lovely. They did not want us to leave. It was only the miscreants from other cities that were involved in all the loot and murder."

Another one added, "The miscreants had gone mostly from Muzaffarnagar to cause trouble."

"Which Muzaffarnagar?" I asked.

"Muzaffarnagar, the city here in Uttar Pradesh," came the reply.

The elderly gentleman took out his smartphone, which he didn't seem to be fully conversant with. He said someone had added him to a WhatsApp group of Derawals, and he kept receiving messages from the group members in Urdu, which he couldn't understand. He asked me if I could help in translating the messages. When I took his phone, I found the messages were mass-forwarded Quranic verses and other Islamic texts. I zoomed in on the profile photo of the person who had forwarded the message and was astonished to see it was none other than a close friend of my father. I showed his picture to the elderly gentleman and asked him if he knew the sender. He did not. The sender and recipient did not know each other but were on opposite ends of a communication chain, bound together by their deep-rooted connection to their hometown. And I, sitting amongst them, was discovering these linkages in the unlikeliest of ways.

I averted the matter of translating the message to avoid causing unease and shifted the topic of conversation to Sati Kewal Ram. He was the holiest saint for the Hindus of the region and had set up base in the village of Bilot near Dera Ismail Khan. The temple still attracts Hindu pilgrims from across Pakistan during its annual fair. Rumour has it that some Muslim women also visit the temple to exorcise evil spirits that have taken control of them.

I had to admit guiltily that despite growing up in Dera Ismail Khan, I had never been fully aware of the importance of Sati Kewal Ram temple for the Hindus belonging to that area. I made a vow to rectify this omission on my next visit home.

I was given a tour of the temple. Before leaving, contact numbers were exchanged. The elderly gentleman said, "Don't forget to invite us to your wedding." One of them started humming a well-known Seraiki folk song that had been conceived and composed in Dera, and had become an anthem of the Derawal community of Delhi:

> *Chann kithaan guzaari ayi raat ve*
> *Maida jee daleelan de vaat ve*
> (Sweetheart, where did you spend last night
> My heart continued finding excuses for your absence)

20

Rose Floating on a Cup of Milk

WHEN I RETURNED TO DERA ISMAIL KHAN LATER THAT YEAR, I MADE it a point to rectify having never visited the original Sati Kewal Ram temple in person. So, one day, I set out early in the morning from my home in Dera on an hour-long journey to reach the village of Bilot. Colloquially known as Bilot Sharif to signify the holiness of the place, it has more sacred sites per square metre than anywhere else in the entire region.

At the summit of a parched hill at the approach of the village, ruins of ancient temples from the time of Hindu Shahi empire still stand, magnificent even in their dilapidated state. Inside the village is the shrine complex of Shah Isa, the Muslim saint from the same era as Sati Kewal Ram, whose devotees gather in large numbers at the time of his annual *urs* celebration. But that day, it seemed rather quiet. From a distance, I saw two women in chadars walking slowly behind a turbaned man towards the entrance of the shrine. Perhaps they were going to make a vow of devotion if their prayers were answered.

I remembered the legend narrated by one of the men I had met in Derawal Nagar, Delhi, which went like this: "Sati Kewal Ram Ji went to Bilot and prepared a *thalla* (mud platform) under a bodhi tree, where he started giving religious sermons. Shah Isa, a Muslim religious leader in the neighbourhood, did not appreciate the arrival of a Hindu saint in the village.

"One day, Shah Isa sent a clay cup full to the brim with milk, which was a message to Sati Kewal Ram that Bilot already had its spiritual needs met and that there was no room for a new holy man. Sati Kewal Ram placed a rose on the surface of the bowl and asked the emissary to take it back to Shah Isa. Upon seeing the rose floating on the milk, Shah Isa recognised the implicit message. It meant that Sati Kewal Ram's stay in the village would be like that of a rose on the surface of milk, making it fragrant but without straining it with extra burden."

I asked a young boy to show me where the Hindu temple was. He offered to accompany me in my car, and we took the road. The condition of the road was deplorable, and I wondered why a village that had attracted so many visitors of multiple faiths for hundreds of years lacked basic infrastructure. Through various twists and turns on the bumpy road, we finally reached the gate of the temple. It was painted light green and on an arch above it, the name of the temple was written in Urdu. The boy who had accompanied me bid me farewell and headed home.

I knocked on the gate of the temple and a man emerged. I asked him if I could see the temple from inside, and after a few questions, he let me in. The temple complex had a big tree in the middle of its courtyard, with branches that shaded the whole place. An abundance of colourful threads were tied around the trunk and branches of the tree; a sight not dissimilar to the dargahs and shrines of Muslim Sufi saints. The manner of making conditional vows of devotion was the same. Around the courtyard, there were several rooms, which the caretaker told me were meant to host pilgrims visiting from afar. A sticker written in Sindhi on the marble tiles of the wall asking people to shut their mobile phones off in the temple revealed that many of those annual pilgrims came from Sindh.

Then the man walked me into the main temple area. Outside of it, there was a platform under a shed which was covered with *ajrak* patterned tiles and mirrorwork. It looked like a mini Sheesh Mahal in itself. Strings of plastic flowers, a variety of energy-saving bulbs and a rotating fan hanging from the ceiling diminished the appeal of this little hall of mirrors. In Urdu the words *"Jiye Laal Ji Maharaj"* and *"Jiye Sati Baba"* were written with glass within the glasswork.

Sadly, the actual statue of Sati Kewal Ram Ji was hidden behind a shiny curtain. The Muslim caretaker who was showing me around said it was for safety concerns.

I went back to the courtyard and stroked the trunk of the tree, an offspring of which was now drawing strength from the soil of Delhi. Here, the original abode of Sati Kewal Ram stood in an obscure lane in an underdeveloped village. His statue sat behind a veil, bereft of its original devotees who had to leave behind their guru, their spiritual master, to go to a land far away where they fought to keep his memory alive. The temple had been deprived of its worshippers and the worshippers had been separated from the temple they loved. The loss was palpable in both places. I had closed the loop by paying homage to each of them.

قومی تہوار دسہرہ سب کو مبارک

ڈیرہ اسماعیل خاں کا شاندار دسہرہ

بھل نہیں سکدا ساکوں ڈیرہ
جیکوں آ دے بھلاں دا سہرہ

یر ملکی سیاحوں نے ڈیرہ اسماعیل خاں کو "ہندوستان کا کاشی" لکھا ہے کیونکہ اس شہر میں مندر بہت چیدہ چیدہ مندر ناگرجی۔ مندر گوردھن ناتھ جی۔ مندر ٹھکر رام واقعہ بھاٹیا بازار۔ مندر مرن۔ مندر مروپاں والا واقعہ محلہ دیوان صاحب۔ مندر رگھو ناتھ۔ مندر گوپی ناتھ واقعہ محلہ بھاٹیار رام مندر کلاں واقعہ رام بازار۔ رام مندر خورد واقعہ بازار سگرانوالا۔ ان کے علاوہ درجن کے قریب مندر تھے۔

مدم ہدی مطلب :۔ دسہرہ سے تقریباً تین ہفتے پہلے دونوں رام مندروں میں رام لیلا ڈرامک سے شروع ہو جاتی تھی۔ رامائن کے آدھار پر سب کچھ ہوتا تھا۔ سینکڑوں نر۔ ناری۔ بچے تو رام لیلا دیکھنے جاتے تھے۔ دسہرہ کے دوسرے دن بھرت ملاپ کا شاندار درشیہ دکھایا تھا۔

سہرہ والے دن صبح سویرے مرد، عورتیں، بچے دریائے سندھ میں اشنان کرنے کے لئے ونے شروع ہونے تھے دوپہر تک دریا پر خوب رونق ہوتی تھی۔ سیوا سمتی کی طرف سے گھاٹ بنایا جاتا تھا۔ سیوا سمتی کے سیوک شہر سے لے کر دریا تک صبح پانچ بجے سے لے کر بجے تک ڈیوٹی دیتے تھے۔ پولیس کا بھی خاطر خواہ انتظام ہوتا تھا۔
دوپہر کے بعد رام لچھمن سروپوں کا چناؤ جمہوری طریقے سے ہوتا تھا۔ ہندو چوہدریوں کی طرف جلیوں کی ایک کمیٹی مقرر تھی جو سروپوں کی انچارج ہوتی تھی۔
ری ہردیال گھلیانی کمیٹی کے سکریٹری اور خزانچی تھے۔ کانجی لضف درجن کے قریب امیروں کے بچوں ریں لاتے تھے۔ جتنے بچے ہوتے تھے اتنے پرچے کاٹے جاتے تھے ایک پر رام اور ایک پر لچھمن لکھا باقی سب خالی۔ ملا جلا کر انہیں ایک لوٹے میں ڈال دیا جاتا تھا۔ کمیٹی کے سامنے ایک ایک رچی اٹھاتا تھا۔ جس کے نام پر رام اور لچھمن کی پرچی آجاتی تھی وہ بٹھا دئے جاتے باقی گھر جاتے۔ شنگھار کرنے والے کانجی اُن کو شنگھار کرتے تھے۔ چار بجے بعد دوپہر ان کو بابو مدر کے تھلہ پر بٹھا دیا جاتا وہاں آرتی اتاری جاتی اور پرشاد بانٹا جاتا۔
چہر سگر پوچند ہتر شاذران سے موروثی چلا آتا تھا وہ اپنے گھر سے پالکی میں بیٹھ کر سروپوں والے دروازہ کلاں پر آجاتا تھا۔ وہاں سے جلوس ہوتا۔

21

Sweet was the Sound of Pashto in Jaipur

DURING OUR MEETING IN DELHI, SHILPI GULATI, DIRECTOR OF THE *Dera tun Dilli* (Dera to Delhi) documentary, had suggested that, since I had Jaipur on my itinerary, I should meet her namesake there, who had been researching the origins and customs of Hindu Pashtuns in India. Hindu Pashtuns? I was gobsmacked that such a community existed in India and thrilled at the prospect of meeting one of their members. I could not wait to find out more.

The person I was going to meet in Jaipur was Shilpi Batra Adwani, the conceptualizer and director of a documentary titled *Sheen Khalai* (blue tattooed dots) on the Pashto-speaking Hindus of

Jaipur. We exchanged messages and decided to meet at Tapri Café one fine morning.

As I waited for Shilpi, Atif Aslam's *Mori Araj Suno* started playing on the café's music system. When she arrived, I greeted her with "*Starriya ma se*" (May you not be tired), as I shook her hand. "*Pakhair raghle,*" (Welcome) she replied with a giggle. Tea was brought in an old-style kettle, accompanied by cutting chai glasses.

Unlike my Dera Ismail Khan investigation which had been on the agenda of my India trip before it had even started, discovering this forgotten piece of history related to the other part of my identity came as a remarkable revelation. Shilpi Adwani and her work on the preservation of the history and culture of Hindu Pashtuns opened my eyes to the mysterious ways in which languages and ethnicities scatter and mix, only to later re-emerge and reveal their roots.

Shilpi is the descendent of Hindus from Loralai (in present-day Balochistan, Pakistan). There was a similarity in the stories of the two Shilpis in terms of growing up with mistaken identities. Just like Shilpi Gulati accidentally discovered that her ancestral tongue, Seraiki, was distinct from Punjabi, Shilpi Adwani also accidentally learned one day that she was not of Baloch origin, but Pashtun.

Both Shilpis heard the language of their forefathers spoken in their homes and learned it growing up without knowing what the language was called! While the majority of Pashtuns are Muslims living in Pakistan and Afghanistan, there are lesser-known Hindu and Sikh communities among them as well.

Like Hindus from other parts of Pakistan, the Pashto-speaking Hindus from Balochistan had to leave their home and hearth behind when India was divided. The majority of these Hindu

Pashtuns settled in Jaipur, Rajasthan. They realised that in their adopted homeland they were a minority within a minority, standing out due to their distinct language, heavily adorned clothes and tribal customs. The women of the community had blue tattooed dots on their skin (*sheen khalai*) due to which they were ridiculed. In Shilpi's documentary some of those women narrate how they tried in vain to scrub off the tattoos to avoid the discrimination they had to face because of them.

The same blue dots that enhanced the beauty of those women in their home territory were being erased to escape derision in a foreign territory. For refugees uprooted from their original homes and looked down upon in their adopted homes, the series of tragedies clung to them like a lasting curse.

Shilpi told me the story of how she became cognizant of her Pashtun roots. It was at her university, Jamia Millia Islamia in Delhi, that she got to interact with some students from Afghanistan and discovered that they spoke the same language as her mother tongue. She was able to converse with them in their language. This piqued her curiosity and she decided to dig deeper to discover her true origins.

One of the markers of her true origins were the heavily embroidered clothes Shilpi remembered her grandmother wearing. These clothes were the traditional attire of Pashtun women, featuring colourful embroidery, mirror and metal work, long sleeves and lots of folds in the skirts. The clothes that the women from Shilpi's grandmother's generation used to wear were now lost, in tatters or lying forgotten somewhere at the bottom of storage trunks. She embarked on a project to find and restore them.

Shilpi went around asking the surviving grandmothers and great-grandmothers among the Hindu Pashtuns of Jaipur if they still had their traditional clothes. She managed to secure some surviving pieces, damaged and moth-eaten as they were. With the help of her husband's expertise in textiles, she set about restoring the clothes, complete with their mirrorwork, metal coins and intricate embroidery. Each dress was a rare piece, showcasing an art form that is no longer in practice.

Shilpi continued telling me her story, switching between Pashto, English and Hindi, as she showed me clips from the documentary on her smartphone. More tea was ordered to wash down the delectable anecdotes, accompanied by Parle G tea biscuits. One of the cups had a cautionary note "*Chai peene se kaale hote hain*" (Drinking tea darkens your complexion) engraved on it.

In one of the clips, an elderly man in Shilpi's ancestral village, Mekhtar, Loralai district, was being interviewed. The man went around the village, pointing to houses and shops that were once owned by the Hindu Pashtuns. He mentioned the names of his Hindu friends from childhood that he still remembered. When the same video was shown to the community elders living in Jaipur, they recognised that elderly gentleman. The childhood playmates were able to see each other on video after seven decades.

The effect of Shilpi's work has been priceless. She not only retraced her family history but also reinvigorated a suppressed and forgotten identity for her entire community, one that they could feel proud of once again.

Very few among the people who witnessed the gruesome events resulting from the Partition of India are still alive. Three generations have started their lives since then. They carry the identities of their new homeland. The ancestral lands they left behind on the other side of the border are, for them, nothing more than inherited memories, a collection of anecdotes, or relegated streams of imagination.

Yet some, like the two Shilpis I met, still venture to awaken these memories among their communities. Their efforts instil a sense of pride in their roots, especially among the younger generations, while establishing an association with the places their elders came from and acknowledging the suffering they went through.

Talk of Partition triggers myriad narratives. It resulted in the displacement and cross migration of 15 million people along religious lines. At the house of Shiraz Husain back in Delhi, his mother recounted the story of her uncle migrating to Karachi at the time of Partition. She recalled the time when her father went to Pakistan to see his older brother after many years, only to suffer the painful shock of not being recognised by him. The older brother had lost his eyesight and, along with it, parts of his memory too.

"This cursed Partition has left behind a legacy of endless pain," she said as her voice quivered and her eyes welled up.

22

It Took You So Long to Come Back

MY TWO-WEEK TRIP TO INDIA WAS AS FULFILLING AS MY HEART COULD have desired. I got to meet my friends, old and new, virtual and actual, who embraced me with warmth and pampered me on their home turf. Every place felt like I was already familiar with it; a familiarity originating from an obscure corner of my latent imagination. On some occasions, that sense of familiarity seemed to be overshadowed by another feeling – something akin to a sense of estrangement from past intimacy.

At every point, my mind blatantly compared every aspect of life – attitudes, mannerisms, speech, smell and sounds – with the way things are in various parts of Pakistan. It was not just me, however. I was asked by Indians how I compared their country with mine. Seven decades after Partition, there is still no escape from the original question: how is the other side doing after the split? Just as people have an inclination to justify the decisions they did not make but inherit, and to find ways of feeling pride in the situations they find themselves in, so are the shape of answers to such questions influenced. But despite the demands of pride to appear better off than one's former partner, one couldn't help but be reminded of a ghazal by Bashir Badr, sung by Jagjit Singh:

Mujh se bichhar kar khush rehte ho?
Meri tarah tum bhi jhoote ho
(You stay happy after parting with me, you say?
Just like me, you are a liar too)

India is an incredibly diverse nation, unmatchable in terms of its variety; it is a melting pot of faiths, with various strands even within those faiths. In many ways, however, our two countries, despite being cut off from each other, have grown similarly over the past three generations.

One concern repeatedly raised in India was the rising wave of intolerance, instigated by the majoritarian politics of Hindu nationalism promoted under the current government. This is not very different from what has happened in Pakistan in the past four decades. The seeds of fundamentalism sown early on after Pakistan's creation and nurtured with unprecedented fervour since the 1980s have now grown into a large tree that keeps bearing fruits of conflict. Is India following the same path?

In the words of Fahmida Riaz, yes, as depicted in her prophetic poem "*Tum bilkul ham jaise nikle*" (You turned out to be just like us).

A comment in a gathering of friends was insightful in this regard. One of them asked, "Which period in Pakistan's history mirrors what is happening in today's India?"

"Zia-ul-Haq's rule of 1980s," came the reply from another.

I had no grounds to disagree. During the 11-year long authoritarian rule of General Zia-ul-Haq, press freedom and democracy were brutally curtailed in Pakistan. Religious and cultural intolerance spread through the society. The rise of ethnic and sectarian violence in later decades, which had a profoundly divisive effect on Pakistani society, is often attributed to the enduring legacy of his rule.

Despite receiving news reports of young men being lynched on allegations of carrying beef, an Indian Muslim friend declared they were better off in an India whose constitution was written by B. R. Ambedkar (a jurist and social reformer from a Dalit caste - the lowest position in Hindu caste hierarchy) and guaranteed equal rights without distinction of caste and religion than they would have ever been in Pakistan.

The reality for everyone is different, though, depending on their identity. When I told a friend from Srinagar how at various places I was mistaken for a Kashmiri, she told me that being thought of as Kashmiri in today's India could have been even more detrimental to my safety than my real identity. Due to the armed insurgency in Kashmir, even ordinary Kashmiris in mainland India are often looked at with suspicion.

On the other hand, I met Pakistani Hindus and Sikhs - Sindhis and Pashtuns - at foreigners' registration offices, seeking asylum in India. It is clear that the two states have failed to give their minorities a sense of security and belonging. The difference is only in the degree and extent, which is used as a measure to compare and compete.

During my trip, I got to converse in English, Urdu / Hindi, Seraiki and Pashto. I met Pashto speakers from Balochistan and Seraiki speakers from Dera Ismail Khan. Despite the growing fanaticism on both sites, what remains unalterable is our intricately intermeshed history. Some may say that the current generation is not interested in the cottage industry created out of Partition-related themes, but to the eye that knows where to look, reminders of Partition and how things used to be before it, are to be found everywhere.

There is remarkable similarity even in our ailments and aspirations. For example, I noticed walls hand-painted with Hindi advertisements offering cures for *bawasir* (haemorrhoids), masculine enhancement and private education. Pakistani wall ads target the same client base. I noticed plaques near hand pumps in Varanasi with names of dignitaries who inaugurated them. Same is the norm in Pakistan. We both love to warm our bodies with *kadak* chai all the year round and cool our throats with lassi in summers.

One could get carried away by the recognisable surroundings and the similarity of our circumstances to forget how unreachable we remain to each other, despite being the closest neighbours. India and Pakistan have been independent countries for three quarters of a century. One wonders, however, if they could have lived together as one, had the country not been divided in 1947. Could communal conflicts still have led to an even bloodier Partition, had Britain left the country intact in the hands of local leadership?

One can spend days and nights speculating these scenarios, but the reality is that nobody knows what would have transpired. Just as it is clear that regardless of one's agreement or otherwise to the idea of Partition, it did not have to be executed in a way that resulted in large-scale carnage. Similarly, there is no denying the fact that the two countries could have learned to live as friendly and respectful neighbours, of which there are plenty of examples around the world.

The current realities demand of the two neighbours to drop their animosities and uplift the lot of their people together. Because, as Jagjit Singh sings further in the same ghazal:

Tum tanha dunya se laro ge
Bachon si baatein karte ho
(You'll face the world alone, you say?
How childlike is your talk!)

The myriad stories one has heard about Indians and Pakistanis opening their homes and hearts to strangers from the other side seem to belong to another age. I had heard many anecdotes of strangers being invited for meals into homes and not being charged for goods and services. For me, the number of such experiences was zero. (This could have been due to my forbidding personality, who knows.) What I experienced in India ranged from exceptional warmth and hospitality from friends to being treated with suspicion by strangers. It included welcoming smiles and apprehensive questions. It included an outpour of bonhomie from Muslims and a cold shoulder from hotel receptionists.

The mood of the people and the regime at the helm is but a function of the current moment. My connection, however, is with the history spanning centuries, and with my South Asian identity that is currently housed within the boundaries of Pakistan but also incorporates Afghanistan and India in its fold. A land where, on my first visit, I am greeted with the welcoming expression of *"Bade dinon baad aaye"* (It took you so long to come back) cannot be foreign to me.

Picture Captions

* 9 7 8 1 0 6 8 4 5 0 8 0 8 *

BV - #0034 - 190525 - C35 - 216/138/10 - PB - 9781068450808 - Gloss Lamination